MORE NEW GAMES

for

'TWEEN-AGERS

Other books by ALLAN A. MACFARLAN, *Director of Recreation, Internationally Known Authority on Children's Games,* and *Lecturer on Recreation and Games:*

CAMPFIRE AND COUNCIL RING PROGRAMS

CAMPFIRE ADVENTURE STORIES

NEW GAMES FOR 'TWEEN-AGERS

MORE
NEW GAMES
FOR 'TWEEN-AGERS

BY

ALLAN A. MACFARLAN

ILLUSTRATIONS AND DIAGRAMS
BY PAULETTE JUMEAU

ASSOCIATION PRESS · New York

Contents

Introduction

MORE NEW GAMES FOR 'TWEEN-AGERS is a brand-new book of new and original recreational activities and fun. It contains absolutely no duplication of either material or games which appeared in the author's earlier book, *New Games for 'Tween-Agers.** A great number of the games have been invented or devised by the author and tested countless times in the field since the other games book was written.

Of the more than two hundred games and versions of games in this book, more than one hundred and ten have been devised by the author and have never before appeared in print, though the author has played and developed them with groups of all ages, not only in Europe but from Coast to Coast in the United States and Canada. All of the games and activities in this book have been tried out by the author in junior and senior high schools, among college and university students and at teacher training colleges; all were accepted as good games and were commended for their gaiety and spontaneity.

Many of the little-known games have been adapted from games which have proved popular with children all over the world.

Nearly all of the games are corecreational and many of them can be played successfully by two to twenty players, so that even the smallest groups will find a wealth of material for their play periods in these pages. Many require little or no equipment, with the exception of a ball of some sort and a few paper markers for the start, finish, and boundary lines.

* Allan A. Macfarlan, *New Games for 'Tween-Agers* (New York: Association Press, 1952).

Recreational leaders will find that nearly every game in this book is suitable for *both* boys and girls. Less than a dozen games are classified *for boys* or *for girls* only. The major reason for this is that the girls of today are fond of rough-and-tumble games and often, in mixed competitive events, the girls prove to be the winners in games which call for skill, patience, dexterity, quick decisions, and speed. A great number of the games require quick thought as well as quick action and call for perception and awareness as well as dexterity and speed.

A glance through these pages will show that almost every game set down can be played *either* outdoors or indoors, a fact which will be appreciated by both leaders and parents in rainy weather or when cold winds blow.

Absolutely no unsanitary games or games which expose the players to physical danger are given a place in this book. Gruesome games, and games which are designed to make some players feel foolish, will not be found in this collection. On the other hand, many pointers on precautions to assure safety and hygiene, which have been gathered and developed by the author while conducting thousands of games programs throughout the world, are given in the text for the guidance of the novice leaders of recreation who use this book.

Practically all of the games in *More New Games for 'Tween-Agers* can be played with enjoyment by children of all ages. While imaginative games and games requiring the use of imagination will be found from time to time throughout the book, it is in the chapters on "Games for Little Folk" that games well-suited for the make-believe period of early childhood will be found. University students and many adult groups have played all of the games in this book and declared them "good fun."

Prehistoric children may have played "Look Out for the Cave Bear!" and "*You* hear it first!" The dawn-age children who played such games best were the ones who lived to become leaders. Versions of Blind Man's Buff were not only played by youngsters when the world was very young but were equally enjoyed by Grecian children only two thousand years ago. Games have been adapted and re-adapted a countless number of times throughout the ages and have become universal in various versions. The Snow Snake Game of some North American Indian tribes is played, without snow, of course, in the Hawaiian Islands, where it is known as *Pahee*, to mention one instance among many hundreds.

It is an indisputable fact that play in its many forms has always been an important factor in the social development and healthy growth of children. Playing good games develops individuality as well as team spirit, sows the seed of true democracy, instills the spirit of fair play and demonstrates its advantages. Through competitive games players learn that they must give as well as take in their association with their playmates, and it is good for them to learn early in life that there must be a certain amount of giving as well as taking in order to achieve worth-while living. Games worth playing have a high moral value. Good sportsmanship is developed, and the practice of fair play and the art of losing games graciously comes naturally with play under efficient leadership.

Games are useful in helping players develop character, patience, self-control, will power, imagination, quick thinking, mental and physical control, concentration, and co-ordination, along with a co-operative spirit. Team games and the fact of playing as a member of a team help to foster *esprit de corps* which proves of value to the players not only in the formative years but later in life as well.

Play provides a valuable emotional outlet for many children, not only backward children, but also bright children who are shy, yet can be drawn out through participation in games.

Based on the proved theory that games which have been tested, re-tested, and enjoyed by many groups of children of all ages are good games, because children themselves are among the world's greatest judges, this book has been written for recreational directors and leaders of all youth activity groups of all denominations; Boy Scout and Girl Scout, YMCA and YWCA, leaders; camp directors; counselors, teachers; physical education directors; parents; and all who direct the play of girls and boys. It is the author's sincere hope that *More New Games for 'Tween-Agers* may prove the key to a new world of games.

MORE NEW GAMES

for

'TWEEN-AGERS

1.

Creative Game Leadership

COUNTLESS books on games have been written over the years, yet it must be apparent to the more experienced leaders of games that so far the surface of games, as well as their adaptation, has only been scratched. One reason for this is that so many games programs are repetitious and the supposed modifications of games follow too closely the basic game patterns which have come down to us through the ages.

A leader with imagination, and it is impossible to imagine a leader without that quality, can work wonders with almost any game, independent of its vintage. An alert leader uses his imaginative ability to become a spectator at a game played for appraisal in his mind's eye. As he watches and analyzes, he detects things which can be eliminated and sees things which can be added to make a good game even better and more acceptable to a wider range of age groups.

All really good games should be fun to play, but if the leader chooses ones which help to develop quick thinking, skill, dexterity, and speed on the part of the players, so much the better. Good games should be easy to play, with a little thought and effort, but not so easy that they offer no physical or mental challenge.

Games were played by prehistoric children; and those who developed alertness, quickness, good hearing and eyesight, and quick and quiet movements were considered so important that they were often taught by the best hunters of the tribes. Such games and the training which was an integral part of the games often meant the difference between life and sudden and painful death to these young people, not only in youth but in later life also in those perilous times. Games are timeless and some have become universal. Choosing such games and adapting them so that they become suitable and clamored for by the youngsters of today presents a challenge to modern leaders which cannot be ignored. A conscientious leader does not even try to bypass the dare because he knows how much easier it is to direct games which the youngsters like to play than ones which are less popular with them.

How GAMES ARE GROUPED IN THIS BOOK. It may be well at this point, while speaking of choosing games, to outline just how the games in this book are grouped and how a leader can get the most out of them. Each chapter is made up of games arranged in a specific category, such as "Tag Games," "Picnic Games," and "Quiet Games," for example. Only a very few games in this original collection are marked *For Boys* or *For Girls* only, because practically all are suitable for play by *both* boys and girls. Girls like to play rough-and-tumble games these days and often excel in them. Only a few games are described as being for boys *or* girls, meaning that these games are best played by groups of either boys *or* girls and not by mixed groups.

Many games are marked for both *Outdoors* and *Indoors,* though a number of them are best played outdoors. In such cases of double listing, indoors is only mentioned in connection with some games to meet rainy weather conditions in camps and play centers which have large recreation halls, gymnasiums, or other large indoor play space available for use in bad weather. The caption at the head of each game first mentions where the game is best played, and then lists the second choice. When the game is strictly an outdoor *or* indoor activity, that fact is stated in the caption. In games which are designated as *Individual-Team,* two or more individual players can compete one against the other, but when more players are available, teams can be formed.

Practically every game in this book, with the exception of those in the "Little Folk" chapters, are suitable for play by boys and girls of all ages, in the *Elementary through Junior High* groups. The suggested selection of games set down for *Senior High School* groups has also proved popular with college and other adult groups. The classification of some games, such as those in the "Picnic Games" group, could have been included equally well in other chapters where activity and fun predominate.

Ideas concerning safety and hygiene in games and similar information useful to play leaders will be found in the next chapter.

IMPORTANCE OF VARIETY IN GAMES PROGRAMS. Games have been classified and grouped under various suitable headings. The variations of a basic game follow the original game, chiefly for convenience of reference. Game leaders know that a frequent change of formation and pace is necessary to assure a well-balanced and successful games program or games period. Some novice leaders have an inclination to lead one game after another with the players in the same formation. This is usually done either because it saves the time and trouble of arranging the participants in new formations or to avoid the disorder among players which sometimes occurs when a novice is leading the games. Leaders should give some time and thought to methods for changing game formations easily and speedily, so that what little time is lost in the change of formation is well repaid by the variation of the games which fairly frequent change of formations permits. Players of all ages soon tire of conventional relay races and too many circle games, which is a good reason why only two or three of such games, at the very most, should be played consecutively, unless the actions in each game are entirely different. The games leader scores when he calls the changes in games before changes are suggested by the players.

LEADERSHIP IN GAMES. A good leader is accepted by the players as a member of the group with the same interests and goal. Teachers realize that real games cannot be successfully taught by the usual schoolroom methods. No child should be coerced to play a game; he should be encouraged to desire to participate.

A successful games program must be kept moving, and while a fairly fast pace should be maintained in order to add to the excitement, variety, and fun, no game should be hurried over or abandoned half way through in an effort to maintain too fast a pace. Any game that a leader considers worth including in a program of games is worthy of the same consideration, trial, and fair play that is developed and encouraged by playing games. All leaders, when trying out new games, should read the play-way of each game thoroughly from beginning to end and fully understand just how it is played before trying to play it with a group. Quite often a brief demonstration of a new game played by a few alert players is the best sort of explanation. Leaders should always prepare even the simplest equipment required for a games program well in advance of the event.

Usually games can best be explained by a leader standing alongside the players in a circle. He can see all of the group from that position and all of the players will hear him equally well. Games should be halted as little as possible by the leader for the purpose of criticizing a player or explaining a point of play more fully. The points of each game should be described or demonstrated, or both, clearly and *before* beginning the game so that all questions may be asked and answered before play begins. While a running commentary by a leader during some parts of a game can prove helpful at times, the remarks should not tend to slow down the tempo of the game or distract the attention of the players.

Various ways of stepping up the tempo of games to assure increased activity for more players will be devised by alert leaders, such as throwing an extra ball or two into play at times or increasing the number of taggers.

Leaders can save time and avoid possible arguments in the process of *counting out* by asking for volunteers for jobs such as being *It*. It can be pointed out that only good sports volunteer for the harder and more exciting roles in a game, such as being *It*, and that volunteer players generally fill them better than players who have been assigned the job by some counting-out system or rhyme.

HANDLING THE COMPETITIVE ELEMENT IN GAMES. The competitive side of games should neither be unduly stressed nor too strongly discouraged. Competition in games is liked by most players and when properly developed and controlled it can be used to advantage. Good leaders rarely stress the winning or losing of games by either individuals or teams. They explain that good sportsmen never boast about their successes: only mediocre ones do that. When a boy, with the candor of youth, remarks to a leader that "Ted surely played a third-rate game of Touch and Go!" the reply of the experienced leader is along the line—"Perhaps, but he did his best and he played like a champion in Border Raid."

There are two schools of thought when it comes to dropping youngsters from a game because they have lost out to better players. The author believes that it is fairer and better for everyone concerned to eliminate players from a game because of a breach of rules or poor play rather than to pretend that they are still in the game by giving them some minor, more or less inactive role from the time that they are actually out of the activity. Sooner or later, usually sooner, even the younger players will learn from other players that they are simply being catered to or babied by the leader. Usually this proves a greater shock to their pride than being ruled out for a fault, which they will endeavor to avoid next time in order to remain in the game for as long a period as possible. There is little point in elaborating on this subject, though some leaders studiously avoid the elimination of the poorer players, even though it is quite obvious to the players themselves that they should be out of the game. One wonders how these leaders manage when directing the various forms of Tag games!

It is usually a good policy to score both individual and team events so that 1st, 2nd, and 3rd places are awarded. In this way everyone will continue the game instead of stopping play when the first player or team wins. This system also gives more players a chance to score, and a player or team making only 3rd place in the first game will be a strong contender for 1st place next time.

While the word "leader" is frequently used to distinguish the person who is actually leading the games, these leaders should always be on the lookout for older or even younger players with a flair for playing games who may make good games leader material. These players should be given the opportunity of leading various games from time to time, with helpful comments from the adult leader when necessary. Quite frequently the temporary appointment of a captain to lead a team or group is the first step in developing juvenile leadership.

MODIFYING, ADAPTING, AND INVENTING GAMES. Although games of a "Let's pretend" nature are often favorites with primary groups, older players as a rule prefer something more tangible than merely pretending to do something. Experienced leaders not only choose games which best suit the various age groups but they also realize that mixed groups where smaller players play competitive games against older and considerably bigger players are rarely successful without some divisions and handicaps to even things up a bit. Although some games in this book may suggest 20 or 30 feet as a suitable distance between the start and finish lines, or as the diameter of a game circle, these distances will be modified by alert leaders to suit the ages of the various players in the different age groups. In fact, distances and boundaries for some games are only restricted by the play space at the leader's disposal.

When space is limited, putting more markers between start and finish lines and having older players return to the starting line after reaching the finish line are ways of increasing difficulties and distance for older contestants. Good action games can always be adapted to offer the challenge and incentive needed to make them liked by players of varying ages. While mentioning the fact that nearly always some simple modification of the average good game can make it more acceptable for various age groups, it is equally true that at times the changes have to be rather subtle. Making such improvisations does not faze an experienced leader. By the use of imagination —one of his most precious gifts of leadership—the adaptation of games comes easily to him. In this way he gets new games from old, and good games become even better ones.

Too often, those who lead children in play or "devise" and revise games to be played by children believe that changing the name of a game is all that is required to have the "new" game gratefully accepted by the players. Younger players may do so, for a brief period, but older and more sophisticated players are not deceived by the subterfuge. Were it not for this juvenile perception, there would be little incentive or reward in really devising games for children and leading them in playing these really new activities. On the other hand, the ambiguous or nondescriptive name of an otherwise worthwhile game may be changed to a really descriptive one in order to establish its category and make it more acceptable to the players. For instance, a leader may ask a group if its members would like to call a game generally known as "Who are You?" to "Alice and the Caterpillar," because the youngsters in the group know that the caterpillar asked Alice that very question. Such a suggestion is logical; there is no pretense of passing off an old game as a new one and usually the children will say, "Yes, let's use that name for our game," thus not only accepting the title and game but adopting it for their own. The author is in favor of such changes when made and agreed on within a play group.

Brand-new games are often born at a moment's notice. Ideas come while watching children, birds, or animals at play. It may not be the actual actions performed by the players at the time they are watched from which ideas for new games develop. Later thoughts, the working of the subconscious mind, and tryouts on a trial and error basis are usually needed to turn out the finished games. Even then, games which may seem to have reached the final stage of development can often be even further improved by a youngster asking, "Wouldn't it be more fun if . . . ?"

Games are also created through mere chance and coincidence, coupled with imagination, of course. The comments on how certain games originated, which introduce a number of games in this book, illustrate how easily intangible thoughts, once triggered by some unexpected sight, sound, or happening, can become tangible play activities.

2.

Assuring Safety in Recreation

SAFETY, and methods for the elimination of all possible sources of accidents while directing games, should be constantly on a games leader's mind. Adequate safety precautions should be taken whether the games are played in the home, camp, schoolyard, or recreation center. The subject is so vast that an entire book could be written on it. Only some of the more common causes of injury are touched on here.

HOW TO PREVENT ACCIDENTS. The avoidance of accidents rests with the leader, and an alert leader must think up ways to prevent the possibility of accidents while games are being played. For instance, it is a needless hazard to play games such as Crows and Cranes and other mass chasing games at one or both ends of a playground with the walls or fences used as boundaries. The use of such boundaries, while convenient, is dangerous. Practically no racing player can stop in a split second, and even if he could there is always the chance that he will be forced against the wall by the impact of the players behind him.

To avoid sprained wrists or worse injuries, the safe way is to draw a heavy chalk line at least 3 feet away from each wall or fence and make the chalk line at each end the finishing point for the chase. Frequently, in confined play spaces, hazardous boundaries exist and the leader's job is to find a way to circumvent them.

Another frequent source of accidents is rough and uneven terrain. The leader may not always be able to level off such play spaces but he can search the ground carefully in order to remove all pieces of glass, loose stones, sticks, and other hazards that are usually found on such terrain. The smoothest part of such land may prove large enough to be used for a limited number of games.

Games that are safe and suitable in some play areas may prove unsafe and unsuitable in others. For example, Hide and Seek, which usually starts with an instantaneous and wild scramble for vantage points in which to hide as quickly as possible, should never be sprung suddenly on any age group standing on uneven ground. A few loose stones lying around or a shallow ditch nearby can cause twisted ankles, severe falls, and other needless injuries which a little forethought on the part of a leader can avoid. A game of Tag started on uneven ground or a wild rush on the sudden shout "Last one to reach that tree is a monkey's uncle!" can also start a blind rush in which youngsters of any age can easily be injured.

Even a simple game of Catch Ball can become dangerous when played on uneven terrain. A player running backward to catch a ball thrown by a leader, or moving fast with his eyes turned skyward, neither thinks of nor sees a small stone in the path which can cause a badly twisted ankle or a nasty fall. The leader should do the thinking *before* such a seemingly harmless game starts.

Such precautions may appear exaggerated, but the term "accident prone" is not just a term conjured up by insurance companies without ample reason. If many adults are accident prone, the number of children in this category are legion. Youngsters of any age, into the late teens, can find weird and apparently impossible ways of injuring themselves even when not engaged in exciting play activities. When one has had to use a keyhole saw to cut a hole in the bottom of a cabin door in a camp to release the foot of an eleven-year-old caught under it, remove a picket from a fence to free a trapped head, and cut through a galvanized drainpipe to extract an arm, the possibility of the endless scope of almost impossible accidents begins to dawn on a leader. After one has hastily sought a tall stepladder to rescue a boy hanging by his T-shirt from

the branch of a tall tree, and has had to saw off a length of
iron pipe in which the inquiring finger of a boy of fifteen was
securely encased, one has no further doubt of the supreme
ability of children of all ages to find ways and means of putting themselves on the spot. The above mention of accidents,
a few out of many equally bizarre, only includes one which
can be blamed on a game. The boy who stuck his finger, up
to and beyond the second joint, into the iron pipe was self-
entrapped in an upright pipe driven into the ground to serve
as a stake in the game of Horseshoe Pitching. A wooden plug
driven into the end of the pipe should have taken the place
of the misplaced finger. The fact that the boy had to be
driven fifteen miles to a doctor, wearing the length of pipe
on his finger, helped to remove him from the accident-prone
class.

Youngsters such as those mentioned above are usually the
ones who get hit on the face or head, at close range, with a
fully inflated basketball or soccer ball in the course of a game
such as Dodge Ball. In this case it is *not* their fault. Care on
the part of the leader to use a softer type of ball, such as an
inflatable beach ball or, if necessary, a heavier type of ball
such as a volleyball—not fully inflated—can prevent such injuries. Another wise precaution is for the leader to see that
certain throwers, carried away by the excitement of the game,
keep outside of the plainly marked throwing boundaries instead of sneaking up too close to assure a hit.

Should a player be hit with the ricochet of a stone while
a group is playing Duck on the Rock, it is *not* his fault. The
leader can easily prevent this kind of serious accident by having the players throw rubber balls, perhaps tennis balls or
volleyballs, at a "duck" improvised from an empty cardboard
carton, such as one in which oatmeal is packed. The target
can vary in size and provide just as much fun as a tin can,
which is sometimes used as the duck instead of a large stone.
The carton suggested offers the same chance for good marksmanship as the tin can and causes little trouble when knocked
from the big rock on which it has been placed into the face

of a player who, unobserved by the leader, has approached too near the rock for a close-up shot. In such cases, a tin can can inflict a nasty wound. A plainly marked boundary around the rock and the statement that any player crossing it to get a sitting-duck shot will be disqualified is another good precaution in this game.

If a player crashes to the ground when struck on the ankle by the swinging bag used in the game of Jump the Bag, it is *not* his fault. The fault lies with a leader who swings a bag which is too heavy, too high and too fast. The bag used for this game should not weigh more than a few ounces and the leader should stoop close to the floor when swinging it around the circle, so that the bag is never more than 5 or 6 inches above ground level as it is swung around the circle. A circle plainly marked on the ground, just behind which the players jump, will prevent the jumpers from coming too close to the leader who is swinging the bag, where they are almost certain to be bowled over by the cord attached to the bag. For their own protection, players who disregard the boundary circle should be ruled out of the game.

All unsafe games which may endanger the players should be eliminated by leaders. For instance, Horseback Wrestling has resulted in many cracked skulls and broken bones. Such injuries are caused not only by a smaller boy being pulled violently from the back of a bigger boy who is playing "horse," but by a boy merely falling from the back of a galloping player when this "game" is being played on hard ground. Other games, such as Bull in the Ring and games which involve running in the dark or running backward, take their annual toll and roll up a high score of fractures and other bodily injuries, many of them serious. Most children, especially older ones, are fond of a certain number of rough-and-tumble games, and a number of strenuous games of that type will be found in this book. Such games, played under careful supervision and by fairly evenly matched contenders, offer no bodily risk to the participants.

Tin cans, which are often as deadly as glass jars or bottles, are sometimes used for various games. The only sort of can which an alert leader will use is one which has been opened by a small hole or holes punched in one end of it. These holes can be covered with adhesive tape to assure 100 per cent protection. If a hole in a can proves large enough for the smallest player to put the tip of his finger into, then that can should be discarded. Fruit juice and evaporated milk cans, which are usually opened by punching small holes on the top, are the safest to use in such games as Kick the Can or any other game where even one player touches the can. Cans with the tops removed or with the tops half opened should be considered in the deadly-weapon category and *never* used in playing games.

When directing Balloon Games in which players hit a balloon, with hands or head, over a rope from opposite sides, slapped faces and collision headaches can easily be prevented by the use of a long rope cut in two. A leader at each end of this double rope can hold the two lengths of it 2 or 3 feet apart. This separates the ropes along their entire length, keeping the players on either side a safe distance apart. Balloons which fall between the two lengths of rope are simply counted out of play and are bounced up by a leader to recommence the game.

How to prevent psychological injury. Hurt feelings in a child can hurt all over! Some ideas for avoiding physical injury and infection have been given, but perhaps the most insidious and lasting injury to children can be caused by psychological hurt. Some sensitive children suffer from its effect for the rest of their lives.

A thoughtful leader will carefully avoid calling a youngster by a nickname which the child dislikes or which may subject him to ridicule. Playmates, for example, may constantly call a stout player "Fatso," but a leader carefully avoids the term and calls the boy by his name. A girl may resent the nickname "Chubby" as much as some fat boys hate the term "Fatso." Such terms should be taboo from a leader's standpoint.

Leaders should studiously avoid referring to a player as being clumsy, even when all of his actions merit it.

A word of encouragement and praise from a leader will work wonders on a self-conscious child and help to discourage players who make fun of him.

Good leaders are always on the lookout for games that may involve the possibility of psychological injury to players. The bad effects of such games make a far more lasting impression on young minds than many physical injuries. Games in which one of the players is made to appear ridiculous are among those which should be permanently struck from the games repertoire of every thoughtful leader of recreation. Such games are introduced so frequently at parties that one is given the impression that they can be safely imposed on groups of older players, who have known each other for a long time, without causing visible hurt or hard feelings. Though this may be true in some rare cases, the recreational leader who drops all such activities from his bag of tricks will gain far more than he will lose from their elimination.

How to prevent health hazards. Unsanitary and germ transfer "games," such as passing a matchbox from nose to nose, or passing an apple or orange held between the chin and shoulder from player to player, are so fraught with the danger of possible infection that they should be strictly avoided by the careful leader of games. Along with such "pastimes," others, such as two players blowing on a ping-pong ball, and into each other's faces, in an endeavor to drive the ball in different directions, can cause infection. Games programs are safer and better without such activities.

Blindfolding one player after another with the same blindfold is another source of probable infection which leaders can circumvent in a number of simple ways. For example, covering the eyes of each player being blindfolded with fresh pieces of sterilized cotton or clean tissue will do the trick. When paper bags are used as blindfolds, their indiscriminate use presents a thrice greater hazard than the regular eye blindfold, as possible infection can come not only from the eyes but also from the nose and mouth. The only sure method of preventing possible infection in this case is to use a clean paper bag only once. Tearing up the bag just as soon as it is removed from a player's head insures its not being used again. A novice leader, new to the vast world of games, may believe that a paper bag may be used twice or even more often without passing on infection. While this can prove true with certain all-round healthy groups, too often infection can strike when a paper-bag blindfold is used for only the second time. The memory of one such infection, caused in a heedless moment, may cause the responsible leader months of futile regret. *Better Safe Than Sorry* is not a mere platitude when applied in the field of recreation: it is a first-class maxim which all games leaders will do well to adopt.

Too often campers become infected with poison ivy when fielding balls or amusing themselves on the edge of a wooded playing field. This can be avoided by a leader having all patches of poison ivy which cannot be killed off plainly marked with stout wooden stakes with rounded tops, painted with red and white stripes.

A child can contract an infectious disease by blowing up a balloon which another child has previously blown up. Although a leader's warning may not prevent such a happening, he can avoid being the cause by not leaving balloons lying around which he intends to use in a games program. Only recently a child died from swallowing a balloon while trying to blow it up. The child passed on before a doctor arrived.

Reading this chapter may lead to the belief that Leadership in Games is a hazardous profession. It is! When one is dealing with the most precious assets in the world, too much care cannot be exercised in safeguarding them. As the author travels from city to town to conduct Games Tournaments or visits camps for the same purpose, the things seen and heard stress the great need for using utmost caution in *all* play activities. Recently a mother told how her son had died from a tumor on the brain, diagnosed by the surgeon who performed the operation as the direct result of a fall from another boy's back, *three years before,* during a Horseback Wrestling "game."

Youngsters are seen in camp hospitals suffering from dislocated shoulders or smashed teeth, because they tried too hard to prevent the "bull" from breaking out of the ring. Other children visited were victims of pinkeye, caused through careless blindfolding during a game.

It is a grave error optimistically to believe that such cases are rare, isolated ones. They occur daily wherever youngsters gather to play. Most of these cases are unnecessary and many can be prevented by dropping all unsafe or suspect games from organized play. Even then, forethought, care, good judgment, and constant supervision of play on the part of leaders are necessary to assure the goal sought by all recreational leaders—safe play. Only great and constant care on the part of each individual leader can assure the mass safety so desirable and necessary in the vast field of recreation.

3.

Running, Racing, and Raiding Games

UNDER THE BRIDGES

FOR BOYS OR GIRLS   10 TO 30 PLAYERS   PLAYED OUTDOORS
ELEMENTARY—JR. HIGH   INDIVID.—TEAM   OR INDOORS

The only equipment required for this exciting and amusing game is two volleyballs or basketballs and a white paper-plate marker 6 inches in diameter.

The players form a circle with an arm's length between players. All face the center of the circle and stand with the legs astride in a comfortable, not exaggerated, position. The plate marker is placed between any two players in the circle. These two players turn and face each other, and the leader gives each of them a volleyball.

On the word "Go!" each player puts the ball on the ground directly in front of the player nearest him and using only the palm of one hand drives the ball under the bridge formed by that player's legs. Both players who are driving the balls run on the outside of the circle and drive the balls under all of the bridges around the entire circle until they arrive back at the starting plate. The fact that the players are traveling in different directions assures their meeting at some point of the circle. This adds to the fun and excitement, especially if they meet directly at a bridge. Should a ball be driven away from a bridge by the ball of another player, the player whose ball was forced out of line must retrieve it and, by the one-hand-drive method, drive it under the bridge that was missed before going on to the next bridge. Players must not touch the volley-ball of another player with their hands. Those who do are sent back two bridges as a penalty, though there is no penalty for a collision between two volleyballs. A ball which fails to go under a bridge must be patted back, always with the palm of one hand, and driven under before the player carries on to the next bridge.

Since one player is forced to use his left hand while circling the players, because it is the hand nearest to the bridges, the fairest way to decide on the winner is to have the bridges circled twice by each player. When a player therefore arrives back at the marker after the first round, he starts around the circle again, running in the opposite direction for the second round. The first player to arrive back at the marker at the end of the second circuit is the winner.

SIT DOWN!

FOR BOYS AND GIRLS   8 TO 20 PLAYERS   PLAYED INDOORS
ELEMENTARY—SR. HIGH   INDIVIDUAL   OR OUTDOORS

The players sit on chairs placed fairly close together in a circle. The chairs face inward and one chair is left vacant at any point in the circle. One player stands in the middle of the circle. When the leader calls "Sit Down!" the player in the middle makes a rush for the empty chair. Before he can reach it, a player from either side of the chair has moved onto it or a player from some other part of the circle has beaten him to it. The player in search of the empty chair must now look elsewhere for it, while the seated players constantly move to fill the one empty chair and try to prevent him from finding a chair to sit on.

The game becomes more exciting when two of the seated players rise and rush for an empty seat simultaneously, giving the seat seeker a brief choice of three chairs.

When the chairless player finally gets a chair, a new chair seeker is chosen by the leader and the game begins again. The choice by the leader is advisable in order to prevent some player from losing his chair too easily, in order to become the new chair seeker.

CATERPILLARS

FOR BOYS   4 TO 10 PLAYERS   PLAYED OUTDOORS
ELEMENTARY—JR. HIGH   TEAM

This amusing race should be carried out on grassy ground free from stones or other impedimenta. There are two boys on a team. A line is marked on the ground as the starting point and another line is marked directly opposite it 30 feet away. The two boys on each team kneel down, facing in opposite directions, with ankles touching, the hands of one boy just touching the starting line. A leader then ties the ankles of the two boys on each team with 2-inch strips of cloth. The right ankle of one player is tied to the left ankle of his teammate and the left ankle is tied to the right ankle of his teammate.

On the word "Go!" each team races to the opposite line, the leading crawler continuing until his partner in the rear calls "Stop!" which he does just as soon as his fingers touch the second line. The race now continues back to the starting point, with the boy who was traveling backward before now leading. The first team to reach the start line wins, as soon as the leading boy's fingers touch the line.

HOW TO MARK BOUNDARIES, MAKE MARKERS AND MARKER STAPLES. At this point, details are given regarding the setting up and marking of boundaries, because the game which immediately follows this information is the first in this book to require such detailed pointers.

Boundary Markers. Definite boundaries should be plainly marked for all games which require them. A start and finish line are most often required, but in some cases side lines must also be marked to keep players within bounds, or markers should be used to prevent players from taking unfair short cuts. Markers are important, since they usually are part of the rules of a game and let the players know that they are playing the game fairly. Without conspicuous, correctly placed markers, games become haphazard and leave room for arguments, unfair practices and decisions. Players who purposely ignore clearly marked boundaries should be ruled out of a game after they have broken the boundary rules two or more times. Markers are so easy to make that there is little excuse for not having an adequate supply on hand when leading games.

Start lines, finish and side lines, circles, oblongs, squares, boundary lines, and other markings can often be marked quite easily with white or colored chalk or even crayon when the games are played on cement, asphalt, wood, or similar surfaces. On sand, clay, beaten earth, and such surfaces a heavy long nail or a pointed stick will mark play areas easily and fairly distinctly. A problem confronts most leaders, however, when their groups are fortunate enough to be able to play games on a lawn or an area covered with grass. Distinct lines may be marked with powdered lime or with one of several white liquid solutions which will not damage the grass, but such solutions are not always available, or perhaps the marking devices are locked in a tool shed when needed. The best substitutes in such cases are markers 12 inches long and 3 inches wide, made from strips of stout, tough cardboard, painted white or yellow to assure visibility. This is advisable for all markers used to define the start and finish points and boundaries required for many games. These markers are easily stapled to the ground with the homemade wire staples described later. Such staples will not harm a lawn and they will assure the various types of markers staying in place. Stout white paper plates and saucers, 5, 6, and 9 inches in diameter, make excellent markers. They may also be had in various colors and can be bought in any ten-cent store very cheaply. Discs cut from heavy white cotton or strong white cardboard also serve very well as markers. Two small holes punched 3 inches apart in the middle of each strip marker or through the center of the bottom of each plate or saucer will allow the staples to be pushed down through these markers into the ground. The distance between the holes will vary according to the size of the tops of the staples used.

Instead of marking an entire circle on the grass, it is much easier to outline it as follows. Fasten a length of strong twine onto two short sticks so that there is 15 feet of twine between them and drive the end of one stick into the ground. Move the other stick around in a circle with the string kept taut and staple markers to the ground at different points of the circle so that the players may line up in the desired circle formation.

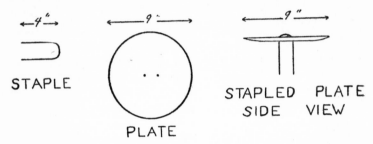

STAPLE

PLATE

STAPLED PLATE SIDE VIEW

When the circle does not require to be of any special size the players simply join hands in a circle formation and back up with the arms extended horizontally with the shoulders until a good circle is formed. The hands are then dropped to the sides and the circle for the game is made. The sticks-and-twine device is also useful in marking out squares and other game formations on the grass. By substituting a piece of chalk for the marking stick, it also makes a good drawing compass for marking circles of any size on a floor or any other markable surface.

How to make Staples. Homemade wire staples can easily be made to hold all types of markers in place. A piece of strong but pliable wire 10 inches long and about ¼ inch in diameter should be bent in two places toward the middle of the wire in order to make a flat-topped staple with a bend of 3 inches, more or less, on top. This bend will give the staple two legs 3½ inches long. The length of the staple legs is best decided by the hardness or softness of the ground into which they have to be thrust. The two legs of these staples are pushed down into the ground through the prepared holes in the paper-plate markers or strip markers mentioned under "Boundary Markers." These staples will serve equally well for holding strips of gauze or paper firmly and safely to the ground. The staples must always be pushed down flush with the top of the marker, so that there is absolutely nothing left above ground for a player to trip over.

The above comments regarding markers and boundaries apply to all games, requiring defined boundaries, which follow.

CAPTURED

FOR BOYS   6 TO 20 PLAYERS   PLAYED OUTDOORS
ELEMENTARY—SR. HIGH   TEAM

This rather rough-and-tumble game will keep the leader on his toes in order to referee well, to see who has captured whom, and to see that the action does not become too strenuous. Two lines are clearly marked on the ground 2 feet apart and from 10 to 20 feet long, according to the number of players on each team. These lines mark the edge of a deep river which flows between them. Ten feet behind each of these two lines another line of the same length is marked to indicate the river bank. Two evenly matched teams are formed with the same number of players, from three to ten, on each team. Each team chooses a captain and a team stands behind each river-bank line, facing the rival team.

When the leader shouts "Action!" both teams approach the river. The members of each team try to grab any unwary player on the opposing team who ventures too close to his side of the river. A player who makes a capture tries to pull his captive across the river and hustle him across the river-bank line. The prisoner may struggle to break away from his captor until he is over the bank line, after which he must not struggle any more and remains on that side of the line. He is out of the game, except for giving encouraging shouts to his own team. Two or three players of the same team may help to carry or drag up the bank a prisoner from the other team. They may also go to the rescue of a player on their own side who has been seized as he tried to grab a rival player and has himself been grabbed. The winning team is decided by counting the number of prisoners taken in the manner described after five minutes of play.

Should players hang back from the river's edges so that no captures can be made, the leaders may decide to let groups of players stage raids across the river in order to capture members of the rival team in their own territory. This is another place where the game can become rough! It can be made less so by not allowing either team to attempt the rescue of prisoners, once they have been taken across the river.

CHIPMUNK CHASE

FOR BOYS AND GIRLS	6 TO 16 PLAYERS	PLAYED OUTDOORS
ELEMENTARY	INDIVIDUAL	OR INDOORS

Markers, about 6 inches in diameter, made from cardboard or cloth are placed on the ground about 8 feet apart in an uneven pattern and all within a square measuring about 50 feet. There is a marker for each player except a cat and a chipmunk. The players, who represent chipmunks, each have a marker for a burrow. Each chipmunk, except the one chosen to lead the chase, stands on a burrow. The cat stands anywhere outside the square, while the chipmunk without a burrow stands anywhere he likes inside the square.

On the word "Chase!" the cat runs after the chipmunk who has no burrow. That chipmunk dodges in and out among the other chipmunks, who cannot be caught by the cat because each one has a burrow. When the chased chipmunk is tired or in difficulties, he runs up to any chipmunk, whistling one little note as a sign that he needs help. At once, the chipmunk that has been asked for help gives up his burrow and rushes off. The cat must always chase the new chipmunk who has given up his burrow to a tired friend.

As soon as a chipmunk is caught, he becomes the cat and a new game begins as before.

HOP ALONG

FOR BOYS AND GIRLS   2 TO 12 PLAYERS   PLAYED OUTDOORS
ELEMENTARY   INDIVID.—TEAM   OR INDOORS

For this game, eight paper-plate markers are placed in a circle about 4 feet apart. Two circles exactly alike should be marked alongside each other on the ground with a space of 6 feet between the circles at the point where they come closest together. The two players, one in each circle, stand opposite a plate marker which has been placed halfway between the circles at any point to indicate the start of the race. Each player stands directly behind a marker in the circle and both players face in the same direction.

When the leader says "Go!" the players hop, with both feet close together, over each marker. Any player who touches a marker with a foot is out of the game. When the players arrive back at the starting marker they continue again around the circle, hopping on the right foot. The third, and final, time around the circle is done by hopping on the left foot. The first player to arrive back at the starting plate after finishing the third round is the winner. In the case of a tie, in the individual version of the game, the leader may have both players hop around the circle backward on either one or both feet, to break the tie.

Hop Along can be contested as a relay race, the first player touching off the next one on his team after finishing the third round, and the race carries on in this manner until each player on each team has had a try.

The race can be made more exacting by ruling players out of the game who lose their balance while hopping or hop on the wrong foot sequence as they circle the circle.

TURNABOUT

FOR BOYS AND GIRLS	4 TO 20 PLAYERS	PLAYED OUTDOORS
ELEMENTARY—SR. HIGH	INDIVIDUAL	OR INDOORS

Two lines are marked on the ground or floor about 40 feet apart. The players line up with toes touching one line and facing the other.

When the whistle blows as a signal to "Go!" all of the players run toward the opposite line, *but* immediately the whistle blows again, they must turn around at once and race toward the line which they have just left. The leader, except when he wishes to end the race at one of the lines, must be on the alert so that he blows the whistle in time to give the fastest runners a chance to turn before they are too close to either line to be able to do so. Players who cross a line after the blast of the whistle are out of the race. The first player to cross either of the two lines—when the whistle does not blow a turnabout signal—is the winner.

The leader keeps his whistle between his lips throughout the race so that none of the players can guess when he intends to blow it.

BORDER RAID

FOR BOYS AND GIRLS	12 TO 30 PLAYERS	PLAYED OUTDOORS
ELEMENTARY—SR. HIGH	TEAM	

No actual equipment is needed for this exciting and somewhat strenuous game. With six to fifteen players on each of two teams, it can be played on a smooth, level area 100 feet long and 50 feet wide. A border line is distinctly marked across the middle of the raiding area, 50 feet from each end. A dungeon 10 feet square, which has no guard, is marked at the end of each area to hold captured raiders. The diagram shows how the play area is laid out and the position of the players on each team at the start of the game.

When the leader shouts "Raid!" the players go into immediate action. Each team tries to capture players from the other side, but they must only be captured one at a time by any one player. Capturing can be done in either of two ways: by tagging an enemy raider when he has crossed the border to take a prisoner; or by the far more daring way of crossing into enemy territory and capturing a player by running a complete circle of any size around him. Of course, a player

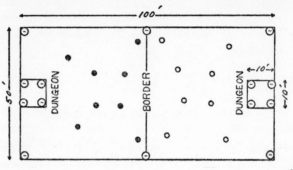

⊖ = MARKERS
●○ = TEAMS

could be tagged twice before completing the capture-circle, or he might have to break off the circling speedily to avoid capture and to return to his side of the line safely, if he can. On being circled, a player is considered a prisoner and his captor is given safe passage back across the border into his own territory. Safe passage means that the captor is allowed to conduct his prisoner through enemy territory and across the border to safety without being tagged on the way. The player does not resist his captor once he is circled and is put into the dungeon to await possible rescue.

All prisoners are put in the dungeon. A prisoner may be rescued by a player from his own side by touching him when he is in the dungeon. Only a prisoner who is actually inside a dungeon may be rescued. He cannot be rescued by sticking a leg or arm outside of the dungeon so that it may be touched easily. Only one prisoner at a time may be freed by one of his own team and only the prisoner touched goes free. The

player who releases one of his team from the dungeon is given
safe conduct across the border until rescuer and rescued reach
their own territory safely.

The game is won by the team which first captures all of the
players on the rival team or has the greatest number of enemy
prisoners in its dungeon at the end of five minutes or more of
raiding.

Each team may choose a captain, and older players especially can work out different strategies which add to the
chances of their team and increase the excitement and suspense of Border Raid.

HANDICAP RACE

FOR BOYS AND GIRLS   4 TO 16 PLAYERS   PLAYED OUTDOORS
ELEMENTARY—JR. HIGH   INDIVID.—TEAM   OR INDOORS

The players line up directly behind one line marked on the
ground, facing another line directly in front of it and 30 feet
away. The handicap in this race comes in because the runners
must race to the other line with the right hand holding the
left knee and the left hand holding the right elbow. On reaching the second line, things do not become easier, since the
runners must return to the starting point with the right hand
holding the left knee and the left hand holding the right knee.
For younger players, the race may end at that point, but for
older players it may be continued as follows. The runners
race back to the second line again with the right hand grasping the right ankle and the left hand grasping the left ankle.
The return to the starting point, which will decide the winner, is made with the right hand holding the left ankle and
the left hand holding the right ankle.

Handicap Race may be run as a regular race with three or
more individual runners, or it may be contested as a relay
race with three or four runners on each team. It is run over
the same course and in exactly the same way as outlined
above except that in relay races the runners run one at a time,
the first runner having completed the course touching off the .

second runner, and so on until each member of the team has run. The first team to finish wins, the leader being on the alert to see that the correct handicap sequence is used by the runners.

CUP RAID

FOR BOYS OR GIRLS   8 TO 20 PLAYERS   PLAYED OUTDOORS
ELEMENTARY—JR. HIGH   TEAM   OR INDOORS

The players are divided equally into two teams. The players of one team stand in a straight line with legs spread wide, but not uncomfortably, apart. The feet of each player, except the two end ones, touch the foot of a player on each side. A cone-shaped paper drinking cup is stood on the ground, point upward, halfway between each player's legs and directly underneath the player. Each player tries to protect his cup from being snatched by a member of the rival team, without moving his feet.

The players on the raiding team rove around the line and try to snatch any cup without being tagged on the hand by the player who is guarding it. Tagging above the wrist does not count but all raiders are out of the game who are touched below the wrist. The raiders can try to snatch a cup from either the front or rear of the players on guard but are handicapped because they must only use one hand with which to actually secure, not just touch, the cup, while the guards may use either or both hands to tag with. Any player who knocks a cup over without actually snatching it is out of the game. Players who lose cones are out of the game.

The leader can either have the guards close in to fill the broken ranks as cones and their defenders are out of the game or let the remaining defenders stay in their original positions with gaps between players. In the latter case, the raiders must not go through or stand in the gaps left in the defenders' ranks, but continue to go around the ends of the line and raid from either front or rear when they are in position to do so.

When all cups have been snatched, the defenders and raiders change places.

Paper balls made of tightly rolled newspaper may be used instead of the paper cups, but the cups provide more fun.

STEADY!

FOR BOYS AND GIRLS	2 TO 10 PLAYERS	PLAYED OUTDOORS
ELEMENTARY—JR. HIGH	INDIVID.—TEAM	OR INDOORS

This is a race with marbles which requires steady nerves and a good sense of balance. For each player, two paper saucers and six ordinary marbles are required.

The two paper saucers are placed on the ground 20 feet apart. The six marbles are placed in the saucer at the starting end. Each player stands beside his marbles.

On the word "Go!" each player picks up one marble with the left hand and places it on the back of the outstretched right hand, anywhere between the knuckles and wrist. He then runs to the second saucer and rolls the marble into it from the back of his hand, without touching it with the other hand. When the marble goes into the saucer and stays there, it counts 5 points for the player. If it misses the saucer or rolls out, only 2 points are scored. The player runs back for the second marble and continues until all of the marbles have been placed in the second saucer. Each player's score is then added, 30 being the top score.

This makes a good team race with two players or more on each team. With a team of two players, one stands at each saucer and when all of the marbles have been placed in the second saucer, the player there carries them back, one by one, to the starting point. The first team to finish is the winner.

4.

Quiet Games

SINCE the first game in this chapter is one requiring a blindfold and leads other games for which blindfolds are used in the following chapters, this seems the logical place to offer some suggestions on the subject. How to avoid the risk of infection when blindfolding players has been covered in the section titled "How to Prevent Health Hazards," in Chapter 2, so the ideas which follow deal only with actual methods of blindfolding.

Gauze bandage strips 2 or 3 inches wide and about 24 inches long make effective blindfolds. Strips of cotton or scarves, in an emergency, may also serve as the outer covering for blindfolds. When blindfolding, care should be taken that the blindfolded players cannot see at all once the blindfold has been applied. This assures fair play for all.

Brown paper bags offer another form of blindfold which is convenient and speedy to use, provided suitable, clean paper bags can be bought or found around the play center. The sizes are usually marked on the bags. The best sizes for most players are the 16 and 18 pound bags, but these are often difficult to find; 14 and 20 pound bags are generally available but the 14 pound size will only fit over the head of a very small player. The 20 pound size bag is too large to prove effective as a blindfold for smaller children. These bags can be adapted by cutting a U-shaped hole about 3 inches wide and 5 inches deep in each *side* of the bag, not in front or back. They can then be pulled down onto the shoulders. When smaller players are creeping or bending forward during the playing of a game, the bag may slip off, so it is best to safety-pin a fold in the back of the bag or even safety-pin it onto the collar or back of a shirt or jacket to assure its remaining in place.

BANKER

FOR BOYS AND GIRLS	4 TO 12 PLAYERS	PLAYED INDOORS
ELEMENTARY—JR. HIGH	INDIVID.—PARTNER	OR OUTDOORS

The number of players in this game is more or less decided by the amount of change which the leader has in his possession at the time the game is played. He does not require much money to get a bank going. Three rather worn dimes, two nickels, and four pennies are all the cash required to set up each banker in business; and a blindfold for each player, to cover the keen bankers' eyes so that they cannot look downward, completes the gear needed. When well blindfolded, the bankers will have to rely on thought and appraising fingers, as they are expected to in this amusing game.

Two rival bankers are blindfolded and placed in front of a table or bench, or seated in front of a cloth spread on the ground. The leader places the coins named above directly in front of each player. The coins should be shaken up and then spread out a little, not placed in a heap. It is now a race between the bankers to see which will first arrange the various denominations of coins in correct stacks. All pennies, dimes, and nickels must be in three distinct piles. Just as soon as a banker feels certain that he has the correct arrangement of coins he shouts "Bank!" The leader then checks the result and the first banker to have the correct arrangement in the shortest time is the winner.

The partner version of this game is even more amusing than

the individual game because the partners are entrusted with six dimes, four nickels, and six pennies between them. The fun for the spectators arises not from the increase of capital but because the partners must consult aloud regarding the denomination of each coin and the correct pile on which each coin must be placed. Frequently it happens that the bankers cannot agree on whether a coin is a penny or a dime and the reason put forth by each banker for its classification is invariably a source of amusement, as the spectators have the advantage of actually seeing the coin being evaluated. It must also be noted here that quite often individual players and partners classify the coins without difficulty because of a difference other than size.

HIDDEN NAMES

FOR BOYS AND GIRLS	4 TO 20 PLAYERS	PLAYED INDOORS
ELEMENTARY—SR. HIGH	INDIVID.—TEAM	OR OUTDOORS

This game, which requires a good deal of thought, is best played when the leader uses a blackboard or a large sheet of paper on which to print in big, easily read letters the sentence which contains the hidden name of a Person, City, Town, or River. Each player should be given a piece of paper and a pencil. The name may be concealed in any long word in the sentence or, better still, broken up between several words, but the letters of each hidden word must follow directly one after the other.

As an example, the sentence *Clothes that are new have no patches* conceals the name of a city in the United States—New Haven. In England, the sentence *The Queen of Sheba sings to keep her spirits up* is considered an ideal and not too easy example which contains the hidden name of a town in England—Basingstoke. The great advantage of such a sentence is that it does not reveal the name of the town even when read aloud or examined closely.

Players should be encouraged to think up clever, plausible sentences which contain the hidden word or words.

COIN DROP

FOR BOYS AND GIRLS   4 TO 16 PLAYERS   PLAYED INDOORS
ELEMENTARY—JR. HIGH   INDIVIDUAL   OR OUTDOORS

The equipment required for this game is a 25-cent piece and a gallon glass jar filled with water. A pail or tub will do when only a few players take part and can stand around and look down into it. However, nothing equals the gallon jar when there are a number of players who remain seated throughout the game. Smaller jars are not suitable for Coin Drop. This is how the game is played.

The leader places a 25-cent piece inside and directly in the center of the jar, which is full of water. The object of the game is for the players, taking turns, to drop a nickel or penny, edge downward, from the surface of the jar so that it will land squarely on the quarter and remain on top of it. Each player can be given two or three tries in succession when there are few players and a number of nickels or cents are available.

It is remarkable how difficult it is, apart from sheer luck, to land the coin squarely on the quarter at the bottom of the jar. It is almost equally difficult when a 50-cent piece is used as a target instead of the quarter. This little game is amusing for the spectators, too, as they follow the dive of the dropped coin to the bottom of the jar. The suggestion that the coin be dropped edge downward is made because it is a little easier to drop a coin onto the target if it is dropped flat from the surface of the water.

THREE OR OUT

FOR BOYS AND GIRLS   4 TO 10 PLAYERS   PLAYED INDOORS
ELEMENTARY—JR. HIGH   INDIVIDUAL   OR OUTDOORS

This quiet game helps to develop quick thinking in addition to providing opportunity for audience participation.

The leader points to a player, then says and spells out any three-letter word, counts up to 10, not too fast, and ends by saying "Out!" when required. For instance, "Man, M-A-N, 1-2-3-4-5-6-7-8-9-10—OUT!" Before the leader reaches the word "Out," the player pointed to must name three words, each beginning with one of the letters of the word given. The words must be in proper sequence and proper names should not be used. If the word is W-A-Y, for example, the three words can be *waltz, about, yonder,* or any other acceptable words in the correct order.

This may seem an easy task, but it is difficult to think fast when working against time. With older players, words of four or five letters may be used, which makes this quick-thought game really hard. In the case of four-letter or five-letter words, a little extra time may be allowed.

BIRDMAN BALANCE

FOR BOYS AND GIRLS	4 TO 16 PLAYERS	PLAYED OUTDOORS
ELEMENTARY—JR. HIGH	INDIVIDUAL	OR INDOORS

Tests such as these are sometimes given to would-be flyers to test their balance and co-ordination. The players stand in a line or circle with about 2 feet between players. The leader asks them first of all to raise their arms forward to shoulder level with the hands held loosely, then raise the right leg, bent so that the knee comes to nearly waist level. The right leg is then lowered and the left knee raised.

The same motions are now carried out with the players standing on tiptoe. Some will pass these tests with flying colors, but there will be fewer successful candidates for wings when these tests are carried out in the same sequence with the players' eyes tightly closed.

Those who lose balance as the tests proceed are asked to fall out, and the last remaining players are the winners. These tests can be made more difficult by the leader asking the players to make various arm and leg motions while standing in the balance positions; the few tests mentioned will be found difficult enough except when the winner has to be found by elimination tests.

STORK BALANCE

FOR BOYS AND GIRLS   4 TO 16 PLAYERS   PLAYED INDOORS
ELEMENTARY—JR. HIGH   INDIVIDUAL   OR OUTDOORS

Those who excel in Birdman Balance should make a good showing in this test too. Players stand in line 2 feet apart with their toes touching a mark on the ground. The leader gives each player a cone-shaped paper drinking cup. The player holds it by the pointed end, leans forward as far as possible and places it slowly on the ground directly in front of him. The player who places his cup at the greatest distance without losing balance or moving his feet either while bending forward or regaining his upright position is the winner. The elimination tests will prove more difficult. The first balance test of cone placing is made while balanced on the right leg only, and the second while balanced on the left leg. Few players will pass if asked to carry out either of these tests while blindfolded.

HEAVE-HO TIDDLYWINKS

FOR BOYS AND GIRLS   4 TO 8 PLAYERS   PLAYED INDOORS
ELEMENTARY—JR. HIGH   INDIVID.—TEAM   OR OUTDOORS

This is a simple form of Tiddlywinks, devised after watching children play that game in England. The Heave-Ho version does not require colored discs of varying sizes and shooter discs for flipping the tiddlywinks into a special cup. For this game, the only equipment needed is a square of cloth or a cloth napkin about 2 feet square, a saucer, and four buttons all alike and about 1 to 1½ inches in diameter.

The napkin is spread out on a table or on the ground with the saucer placed directly in the center of it. The four players stand around the table, or sit on the ground when the cloth is on the ground, one at each corner of the napkin. The first player to start puts his button on his corner of the napkin. Then he holds the point of the napkin between his thumb and forefinger with the button almost touching his thumb. Now, with a slight, sharp upward jerk of the napkin, which must not move the saucer, he tries to flip the button into the saucer.

Some buttons will not reach the saucer, some will fly over it, but only a few buttons will go into and remain inside the saucer. Each button which stays in the saucer scores 5 points;

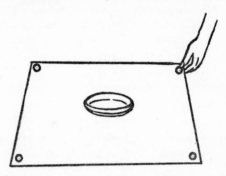

a button which goes in and jumps out counts 2 points. Players take turn about at flipping the button, and the first player to gain 30 points is the winner. For team play there are two players on each team. Players may be given two or three buttons each, instead of only one, and may shoot two or three times in succession, if the leader wishes.

Players may sit or kneel when the napkin is on the ground. To make this game easier, a paper saucer may be used instead of a china one; it is much more difficult to make the button stay in a china saucer, however, and the use of one adds to the fun.

MARINE BANK

FOR BOYS AND GIRLS   2 TO 12 PLAYERS   PLAYED OUTDOORS
ELEMENTARY—JR. HIGH   INDIVIDUAL   OR INDOORS

The scanty equipment needed to put the bank in business is one large pan or tub filled with water, a china saucer, and a dozen 1-cent pieces. Nickels or dimes can be substituted by affluent organizations. Should a china saucer not be handy, a flat paper saucer or plate about 5 inches in diameter will serve quite well and float long enough for the playing of a number of games. A paper saucer or plate can be rubbed with oil, painted, or lacquered so that it will be water repellent. The great advantage of a china saucer is that it makes the game considerably more difficult.

The tub is placed in the center of a 10-foot circle, marked on the ground, and the saucer is floated on the surface in the middle of the tub. The players stand just outside the circle and each player is given a coin. The players try to throw them so that they will land in the floating saucer, which is the "Marine Bank," and stay there. When a player becomes a "depositor" by banking a coin, he scores 5 points, and another 5 points is added for each additional deposit made. The players take turns at tossing the coins unless there are only a few participants; then each player may toss three coins in succession. The scoring is the same as the point system mentioned above. Care should be taken that no water is allowed to gather in the saucer, as it proves too helpful to would-be depositors. The coins, the large majority of them, on the bottom of the tub can be retrieved at the end of each game by a snorkel-equipped leader. The coins should be carefully dried before using them again.

The difficulties in this game, which soon become apparent, can be increased if necessary by marking a bigger circle around the tub to increase the tossing range, or by having the players who manage to make high scores with their right-hand tosses throw the coins with the left hand.

UNFAMILIAR QUOTATIONS

FOR BOYS AND GIRLS	4 TO 20 PLAYERS	PLAYED INDOORS
JR. HIGH—SR. HIGH	INDIVID.—TEAM	OR OUTDOORS

In this literary contest, the leader tries to mislead the *literati* by quoting what are apparently familiar quotations. Quite often the supposedly familiar author of the quote actually turns out to be as unfamiliar as the quotation. This situation arises chiefly because Milton can be mistaken for Shakespeare at times, Shaw's cynical sayings can be attributed to Wilde, while the surprising Cervantes can easily be mistaken for an ultramodern occasionally, despite a hiatus of nearly four hundred years. Most of the quotes used by the leader should at least appear to be fairly familiar in addition to being brief and, whenever possible, complete enough to be easily identified by the phrase quoted.

The quotations can be taken from well-known plays, poems, or books, not forgetting the greatest book of all, which is a living source of inspirational exposition. A leader in the course of this game can impart much information—unobtrusively, of course, as all real leaders do—and at the same time create a lasting interest in famous authors and their works by selecting astonishing, striking, and thought-provoking examples of their art. Humor, wisdom, drama, epigrams, and home truths can all find a place in a well-balanced quote session. Many of the players will be willing and able to add to the verbal feast.

Quote sessions should not last more than ten minutes or so and they must be kept moving at a fairly brisk pace. It is better to stop when interest is at white heat rather than prolong the period until the fire of interest begins to wane. It is also recommended that antiquated quotes and those which lack some special interest be avoided. Another important point in making these sessions repeaters, by request, is to make them tricky by jumping from author to author and poet to poet before the group is able to become well acquainted with their style. The fact that the style of some of the most famous quotables are surprisingly similar also offers considerable scope for misleading even the best-informed.

Every leader has some favorite quotes which he may wish to use and there are literally thousands of wise, timely, magnificent, breath-taking examples lying in wait between the covers of a number of 35-cent and 50-cent paper-cover books which deal entirely with quotations from all sources. The few examples which follow have been taken haphazardly from memory's treasure chest. In some cases it is not easy to place the author; in others, the quotations of long, long ago might easily have been written by a sophisticated modern, while a few of the author's choice are set down for their sheer loveliness.

One last word before getting down to actual quotations. This game can be made still more instructive and interesting by asking the participants to name not only the author but the source of the quotations. When the player who has recognized the quote and author but cannot place the source has had his try, the others in the group may have theirs too, by a show of hands. First hand up, first chance to shine.

The following quotations come from Miguel de Cervantes, blamed by Byron, because of his satirical romance *Don Quixote*, for having "smil'd Spain's chivalry away": *Honesty is the best policy. Rome was not built in a day. Mum's the word. Birds of a feather flock together. Out of the frying pan into the fire. A wise man does not put all his eggs in one basket. Thank you for nothing! Fore-warned fore-armed. Every man for himself. Walls have ears.*

Alexander Pope said: *A little learning is a dangerous thing. To err is human, to forgive divine. For fools rush in where angels fear to tread. Damn with faint praise. I cannot sleep a wink. Some praise at morning what they blame at night.*

Quotes of note from various sources:

Ability is of little account without opportunity: Napoleon.

God gave us memory that we might have roses at Christmas: J. M. Barrie.

Where ignorance is bliss, 'tis folly to be wise: Thomas Gray.

'Tis a long road knows no turning: Sophocles.

Hitch your wagon to a star: Emerson.

God helps them who help themselves; and *Left holding the bag:* Benjamin Franklin.

It is later than you think: Old English sundial.

Imagination is more important than knowledge: Albert Einstein (on science).

Ready money is Aladdin's lamp: Lord Byron.

They also serve who only stand and wait: Milton.

A lifetime of happiness! No man alive could bear it: it would be hell on earth; and *Youth is a wonderful thing. What a crime to waste it on children:* George Bernard Shaw.

What is a cynic? A man who knows the price of everything and the value of nothing: Wilde.

I am a part of all that I have met; and *In the spring a young man's fancy. . .:* Tennyson.

William Shakespeare gave us: *The people are the city. Thy wish was father to that thought. And all my best is dressing old things new. He jests at scars that never felt a wound.*

> *My words fly up, my thoughts remain below:*
> *Words without thoughts never to heaven go.*
>
> *This happy breed of men, this little world,*
> *This precious stone set in the silver sea. . . .*

Keats, master of implication, gave us:

> *Charm'd magic casements, opening on the foam*
> *Of perilous seas, in faery lands forlorn.*

Biblical quotes, from the Old and New Testaments. All of the few quotations, from the thousands that might be given, are taken from the Bible, though some of the listeners during the quotes session may read Cervantes and Shakespeare into a few of them: *A man after his own heart. How forcible are right words. They shall see eye to eye. Hope deferred maketh the heart sick. The borrower is servant to the lender. I am escaped with the skin of my teeth. Speak to the earth and it shall teach you. If a house be divided against itself, that house cannot stand. Labour of love. Wherein thou judgest another, thou condemnest thyself. Watchman, what of the night?*

An interesting quote to interject after some biblical quotations have been given, and the words of other authors are being given, is the following: *Government of the People, by the People, and for the People.* Some, at least, in the group

will "know" that these are the original and memorable words
of Abraham Lincoln. They will be surprised to learn that they
are the words of Wycliffe, used in his General Prologue of the
Bible's first English translation, published in the year 1384.

The most suitable quote, as a finale, is probably: *He
wrapped himself in quotations—as a beggar would enfold himself in the purple of Emperors:* Kipling.

WHERE AM I?

FOR BOYS AND GIRLS	2 TO 18 PLAYERS	PLAYED INDOORS
ELEMENTARY—SR. HIGH	INDIVIDUAL	OR OUTDOORS

This game is played in various forms by children and
grownups alike all over the world. This is not surprising when
one considers that its scope is world-wide. Those who play it
for the first time are frequently astonished at the ease and
speed with which some young players can locate someone who
may be hidden in one of the far corners of the earth.

The leader decides where he wishes to be then asks, "Where
am I?" and need only reply "Yes" or "No" to the questions
asked by the players. Wise players narrow the scope instantly
by asking "Are you in America?" or a similar question which
helps to place the country at once. Clever thinking followed
by clever questioning on the part of some players will soon
narrow the field until the hidden person is discovered, whether
he be in a pyramid in Egypt or on the steps of the White
House in Washington.

As an example of what can be done in this game, twenty
children between the ages of ten and twelve "found" one girl
behind the railings of the Louvre Museum in Paris, in less
than three minutes and after only sixteen questions had been
asked by the players. As a rule, the field should be considerably limited for younger players.

WHERE DO I COME FROM?

FOR BOYS AND GIRLS   2 TO 20 PLAYERS   PLAYED INDOORS
ELEMENTARY—JR. HIGH   INDIVIDUAL   OR OUTDOORS

There are few limits to this game except the actual knowledge of the players regarding the peoples, customs, trades, natural history, and games of other lands.

The leader asks any player the question, "Where do you come from?" The player says, "Where do I come from? I will not tell you the name of my country, but I wear a silk robe where I come from." The leader asks the players to carry on from there and the answer which they have to go on offers several wide choices for guessing. Silk robes are worn in other countries beside India, Japan, and China. A player may say, "There are many poppies in the fields where I come from." This, too, offers a wide guessing range. When this sort of answer is given, any player may ask for another detail in order to help to place the country which is being sought. Apart from answering such questions, the player being questioned need only answer "Yes" or "No."

Answers to the first question—"Where do you come from?"—should not tell too much. For example, a player might state, "I eat sukiyaki where I come from." A player with some knowledge of foreign foods will quickly guess that the person who mentioned sukiyaki comes from Japan. Should the player whose country was to be guessed have said, "I play the samisen where I come from," it is less likely that his country would have been placed as Japan.

The author has discovered that a player's imagination and knowledge of natural history may carry him far beyond the limits of mere countries. One girl remarked during a game conducted by the author, "We have the biggest animals in the world where I come from." The players who guessed India were surprised to learn that they were wrong. Then an alert player who remembered that the African elephants were bigger than the Indian ones placed the girl's country as Africa.

When she said that the answer still was wrong she was asked for further details. She then said, "I wear no clothes where I live." Eventually she had to explain what should have been clear in the first place. As whales are the biggest animals in the world, she had become a mermaid and lived in the wonderful realm of the sea!

PICTURE MY THOUGHTS

FOR BOYS AND GIRLS   4 TO 20 PLAYERS   PLAYED INDOORS
ELEMENTARY—SR. HIGH   INDIVIDUAL   OR OUTDOORS

The leader sits in front of a group and thinks of a country which he knows quite well. It may be America, Canada, England, France, Italy, or Japan. When he has decided on the country he puts his mind's eye to work and visualizes a specific place, scene, and time of year.

He then says, "I am in Canada. There is a great building in front of me. In front of it I see tall men wearing scarlet

and blue dress. Which city am I in and what scene do I see?"
or "I am in a picturesque city, in a strange boat. There are
buildings on both sides of me and in front of me; as the boat
glides along, I see a covered bridge. Where am I and what
scene is in my mind's eye?" Again, the leader may state, "I
stand under cherry blossoms; I see a river and a monument
of some sort. Where am I? What do I see as I look around
me?" Many questions such as these may be asked about different countries and cities. For older groups, the questions may
be less obvious. The reader will have deducted that the first
scene was laid in front of the parliament buildings in Ottawa,
with the Royal Canadian Mounted Police on guard. The
second scene is harder to place. A player who suggests that
the leader is in a gondola in Venice can be as correct as one
who believes that the scene is laid on the River Arno in
Florence. The third mind picture suggests Washington, D.C.,
so strongly that there is little chance of error.

The leader asks the first player who raises a hand to indicate the fact that he believes he knows where the leader is,
to describe, very briefly and without naming the city or town,
what the leader had in mind. Only at the very end of his
description does this player name the building or buildings,
if he can, and also name the city. These mind pictures give
the players a chance to develop storytelling ability and permit
those who know a place well to paint an interesting and in-
formative word picture of it. Older players, especially those
who have traveled abroad, should be given a chance to lead
this quiz game. Those who lead may either be given the
chance to prepare an outline of a few places in advance or
be called upon to launch into the descriptions on the spur of
the moment.

The possibilities and scope of this game make it suitable
for players of all ages. Senior high school students who have
glibly word-pictured the Louvre, a scene on the Grand Canal,
or the Golden Horn may find themselves at a loss for both
words and knowledge when they are confronted with the
Temple of the Eye at Katmandu.

WAXWORKS

FOR BOYS AND GIRLS	4 TO 12 PLAYERS	PLAYED OUTDOORS
ELEMENTARY—SR. HIGH	INDIVID.—TEAM	OR INDOORS

This game is best played after a leader has told the players something about Madame Toussaud's remarkable waxwork museum and some of the many famous and not so famous wax figures which are found there. In such a museum even grownups often make the mistake of asking policemen, cleverly made of wax, how to find a certain exhibit, or asking little wax children, who look frightened, if they are lost. The game Waxworks was born while the author was watching English children take up imitative poses in front of some of the lifelike wax figures mentioned.

Individual players or rival teams with two to six players on each can contest. Each team is asked to portray some well-known character, or a group of two or more famous people, each team taking turns at impersonation. The persons chosen are the personal and secret choice of each individual player or team. The figures may be Oliver Twist, Cinderella, Napoleon, Peter Pan, Beauty and the Beast, or others, from history, storybook, or fairy tale. The players may be allowed to use handy objects, such as a scarf, tablecloth, cane, umbrella, and so on, to add to the effect but actual "dressing up" is not permitted, as too much time is lost when costumes and hard-to-find props are introduced. The team which is not doing the impersonating is asked to look in the opposite direction for a few moments while the figures take up their positions.

When a leader says "Ready," the team which is doing the guessing turns around and goes to work. Its task may not be easy, because the players have disappeared and strange, strained figures have taken their places. Perhaps Sitting Bull or Peter and Wendy in the act of flying are waiting for their identities to be thought out or guessed. The guessing team may be given two minutes and three guesses to decide what persons are represented.

An extra amount of fun is added when any player on the guessing team who laughs or even smiles at any figure made by the mimes is ruled out of the game. To even things up, the guessing team may make any remarks it likes about the "waxworks." Should any figure smile because of comparisons made, or remarks about wiggly ears, that player is out of the game.

When older groups play, it is well to have one or more independent and, if possible, unbiased judges to decide on the teams putting on the best show.

CHING-CHANG-POK

FOR BOYS AND GIRLS   **2 TO 14 PLAYERS**   **PLAYED INDOORS**
ELEMENTARY—JR. HIGH   **INDIVID.—TEAM**   **OR OUTDOORS**

This little game was used in Old China for counting out. It is played in the same way as *Jan-Kem-Po* is played in Japan only in this, the author's, version there are new words and hand signs. It can be called either by the Chinese name or Earth, Water, Fire. This is how it is played.

> *Earth* is indicated by opening the hand flat, palm downward.
>
> *Water* is shown by letting the fingers and thumb hang downward, with the back of the hand facing forward, to indicate falling water.
>
> *Fire* is represented by raising the fingers and thumb, with the fingers pointing upward and the palm of the hand facing forward, like tongues of shooting flame.

The scoring is done in this way:

> *Earth* drinks the *Water*, and wins.
> *Water* puts out the *Fire*, and wins.
> *Fire* scorches the *Earth*, and wins.

Two players face each other, 2 paces apart, holding their right hands closed and at waist level. One player says "Go!"

and they bring their clenched hands from waist level up to shoulder level, then down to waist level again, three times, each player making the sign which he has decided on, on the third time down. To regulate the speed, so that each player can keep the same time, each player should say, aloud, *Ching-Chang* as the closed hand is raised rather slowly to shoulder level and *Pok* as the closed fist is brought swiftly down to waist level. The hand of each player is opened at waist level and at the same moment on the third *Pok*, each player ending the movement in one of the three signs. The signs made decide the winner but if both players make the same sign, which happens fairly frequently, neither player scores and they try again from the beginning. The winner is best decided by the result of three tries, not counting ties.

Two teams of four or more players can compete in this game. A leader is chosen for each set of three tries and helps to decide, secretly, on the sign to be made by all members of his team, in an effort to beat the rival team.

PARTNERS

FOR BOYS AND GIRLS	2 TO 12 PLAYERS	PLAYED INDOORS
ELEMENTARY—SR. HIGH	INDIVID.—TEAM	OR OUTDOORS

This game covers a lot of ground, which makes it suitable for groups of different ages where the field of knowledge of a group is fairly evenly matched. The partners to be paired are people and things so closely associated that they suggest partners, without a lengthy flight of imagination. When one person or thing is mentioned, the thoughts quickly fly to the other. For instance, a leader or player who says "Eve" will not be long in spotting a dozen hands raised to supply the name of her dispossessed partner.

There are various ways to play Partners, based on the group age of the participants. For instance, with a younger group when a famous sword such as *Excalibur* is mentioned, the suggestion of King Arthur as a partner is cheerfully accepted. Should an older player mention the same partnership and a better-informed player suggests *Balmung,* the latter answer should be accepted as the most appropriate one, as it pairs two famous swords, even though one is less mythical than the other.

When partners are asked for Dr. Watson, Ruth, Wendy, Sancho Panza, Oliver Twist, and Huckleberry Finn, they will not be long in being found. In such cases as Oliver Twist, when Charles Dickens is named as a partner there is little reason why he should not be accepted. These few illustrations hint at the vast field to be drawn on.

History, geography, famous people, cinema, literature, and sport all supply suitable material for partners. A game may be entirely devoted to men and women pairs who suggest partners; books, history, and plays supply abundant examples. A leader is useful in the role of moderator or he may supply the names of people and things to be paired.

BOX OF SECRETS

FOR BOYS AND GIRLS	6 TO 20 PLAYERS	PLAYED INDOORS
JR. HIGH—SR. HIGH	INDIVIDUAL	OR OUTDOORS

This is a good surprise event which will help promote extemporaneous speaking, in addition to providing the orator with an opportunity for a display of swift thinking, use of rhetoric, and the exploitation of whatever flair for the dramatic and humorous he possesses.

The leader hands a player a small closed box and asks him to tell a story or make a speech which will coherently connect all of the articles in the box in an interesting and amusing manner. The box should contain three small, varied objects. A different set of articles is provided for each speaker. He opens the box and names the contents aloud, then starts the story immediately. The narration should not take more than two or three minutes. The story should connect the articles found in the box in some logical way, even though they appear to have neither logical nor recognizable relation.

The sets of three articles can be varied to suit the imagination of the leader who places them in the box in advance, prior to calling each speaker. Considerable additional fun can be assured by a leader putting articles in a box for certain speakers which can stir memories of the speaker, and audience, or ones which the speaker called on can use most effectively as a basis for the most amusing dramatics, heroics, and melodramatics imaginable. A few suggestions for some article trios follow: a pencil, piece of string, woman's glove; handkerchief, piece of chalk, key; powder puff, fan, match; a canceled stamp, hairpin, button; small flashlight, pair of scissors, aspirin tablet; flower, shoelace, earring; and so on. The number of suitable articles and the combinations in which they can be introduced into a tale or talk are almost numberless.

The scope offered for a really funny, seriocomic, or tragic tale is so great that no speaker who possesses imagination need side-step conventionalities in order to create a story suitable for telling before any audience. Points may be awarded to decide the winner, or the champion may be chosen by audience applause.

GOOD MORNING, MARK!

FOR BOYS AND GIRLS	6 TO 20 PLAYERS	PLAYED INDOORS
ELEMENTARY—JR. HIGH	INDIVIDUAL	OR OUTDOORS

This is a sort of detective game which gives the players a chance to see how good they are at detecting voices and telling to whom they belong.

The players stand or sit in a group and the voice detective turns his back toward it. The leader points to a player in the group and he has to say "Good morning, . . . ! using the "detective's" first name. The detective replies "Good morning, . . . ! naming the player who has spoken, if he can, to show that he has recognized the voice. For the first round, at least, unless the players know each other very well, players should use their natural voices.

When the detective, without turning around, names the speaker correctly, the leader tells him so and then points to another player to give the greeting. Each time the detective names the player who has spoken, he may continue for four or five more greetings, or until he fails to guess the speaker correctly. When the detective guesses wrongly he changes places with the speaker whose voice he did not recognize.

As a variation of the game, after playing it straight for a number of times, the leader may ask the players who give the greeting to disguise their voices in order to make the work of deduction more difficult.

Players may be surprised to learn that some voices, perhaps their own, are distinctive and cannot be successfully disguised and that some voice detectives have ears which are difficult to deceive.

DEER AND RABBIT

FOR BOYS AND GIRLS	2 TO 10 PLAYERS	PLAYED INDOORS
ELEMENTARY—SR. HIGH	INDIVIDUAL	OR OUTDOORS

This stunt will puzzle and amuse the most astute senior high school students. Perhaps the best explanation of what happens may be explained by kinesthesia. The players are paired off and work together as partners. One player is given a penny with a 12-inch length of light string fastened to one edge of it by a piece of adhesive tape or a spot of glue. The string should be attached so that the coin hangs vertically. To help the experiment, it is best to make one or two ordinary knots tied very closely together on the free end of the string.

The player with the penny holds the knot on the end of the string between his thumb and forefinger. His partner holds out a hand, flat and palm upward, about waist level. The experimenter then suspends the penny so that it hangs an inch or two above the outstretched palm. Now, he and his partner should both think hard about a deer, remembering that a deer usually moves in a straight line when in a hurry. With this thought firmly in both minds, the coin will soon start to swing straight forward then back, in pendulum fashion. The interesting point about the coin movement is that the player

holding the string by the knot on the extreme end tries hard
to make absolutely no movement that will set the coin in
motion. His partner may not believe this until promised that
he will have a chance to use his mental control when his turn
comes to suspend the coin.

When the coin is swinging back and forward, the experimenter asks his partner to co-operate with him in concen-
trating on a rabbit, which usually runs in circles, in order to
have the coin circle like a rabbit instead of swinging in pendulum fashion. After a moment or two of concentration on the
part of both players on a rabbit running in a circle, the coin
begins to swing in a circle. As both continue to think rabbit,
the coin will swing in an ever increasing circle. By changing
the thought back to deer again, the circle will diminish and
the coin will go back to the pendulum swing. The coin changes
hands at this point and the assistant becomes the operator.
The coin responds wonderfully well to some partners and
poorly to others.

5.

Picnic Games

CATCH AND RUN

FOR BOYS AND GIRLS   5 TO 20 PLAYERS   PLAYED OUTDOORS
ELEMENTARY—SR. HIGH   INDIVID.—TEAM

This fast and exciting game only requires a partially in-flated volleyball or any other large, soft rubber ball and a number of white paper-plate markers 6 inches in diameter. There must always be one marker less than the number of players in the circle and one marker to show the center of the circle, as indicated in the diagram. The markers are evenly spaced in a circle about 30 to 40 feet in diameter. The players stand around the central marker, fairly close to and facing it. A leader, holding the volleyball, stands beside the marker in the middle of the circle.

To start the game, the leader throws the ball high and straight up into the air, above the center marker. As the ball falls, all players try to catch it. Just as soon as a player catches it, all the others make a rush for the markers. A player who runs for a marker before the ball is actually caught can be ruled out of the game. The player who catches the ball may throw it at any player but the throw must be made from the spot where he caught the ball. A player who is hit below the waist is out of the game and the thrower has a marker in the circle. He stands with one foot on it, as the other players are doing at their markers. The players then return to the middle of the circle and the leader removes a marker before throwing the ball up into the air again. The *catch* in this game, apart from the title, is because there must always be one marker less than the number of players who try to catch the ball. In a rush for markers, after the ball has been caught, two players often run for the same marker. When one player reaches it ahead of the other and claims it by putting his foot on it, the other player must run for another marker which has not been claimed. The last remaining player is the winner.

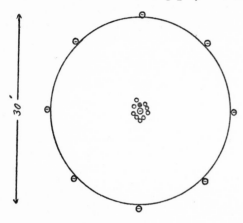

⊖ = MARKERS
● = LEADER
○ = PLAYERS

As a team game, Catch and Run is played with two teams of equal size competing. It is a wise precaution to identify one team from another in some easily visible way, such as having the members of one team wear handkerchiefs around their arms. This will prevent the catcher from putting one of his own team out of action. The winning team is the one with the most players on markers at end of game.

CRAWLY

FOR BOYS AND GIRLS   **4 TO 16 PLAYERS**   **PLAYED OUTDOORS**
ELEMENTARY—JR. HIGH   **TEAM**

Here is another original and amusing game to be played on the grass, after it has been carefully inspected to be certain that it is free of glass and stones. The grass will save wear and tear on the knees and jeans of the players.

Teams, with two players in each, line up directly behind a starting line. Opposite, and at a distance of 40 feet, another line is plainly marked on the ground. The players on each team go down on hands and knees, side by side, with one player directly alongside the other. There should be a distance of 3 feet between teams. The fingers of all players should just touch the starting line.

When the leader says "Go!" the player on the left of the team crawls completely around his teammate as quickly as possible, without touching him as he circles. His circle should end directly in front of and a distance of about 2½ feet from his teammate. When the player behind him can just touch *both* heels he calls "Stop!" and then, in his turn, circles the player in front of him, also trying to stop about 2½ or 3 feet directly in front of him. Players may stretch forward in order to be able to reach the heels of the player ahead of them but must not advance to do so. The player in front must not stretch his legs backward if the player in the rear cannot reach them but he may back up so that he is not out of reach. The race continues as described until the leading player of each team crosses the finish line, and the first player to do so decides the winning team.

The leader who referees this race will have to keep an alert eye open to see that no player stretches his legs back beyond the normal crawling position in order to make it easier for his partner to touch his heels. A player who does this more than once can be disqualified, as it is a simple matter to crawl a foot or two, backward, of course, to be within reach of his teammate's touch.

A variation of this race is to have each player only crawl for one half circle, crawling from behind to just in front of his partner, without circling him.

ROW BALL

FOR BOYS AND GIRLS	12 TO 20 PLAYERS	PLAYED OUTDOORS
ELEMENTARY—SR. HIGH	TEAM	OR INDOORS

Two teams of six to ten players sit in two parallel lines 4 feet apart, each team facing in a different direction. The feet of each team's players should just touch the seat of the jeans of the teammate directly in front of him. The first player in each line can keep his legs extended in front of him, since there is no teammate ahead of him. In this position, teams sit directly opposite each other, as shown in the diagram, with the right hands in the lane between the teams. The other hand must be kept on the left-hand side throughout the game. The leader staples a cloth marker to the ground, or marks a small chalk circle on the floor, in the middle of the lane and halfway from each end.

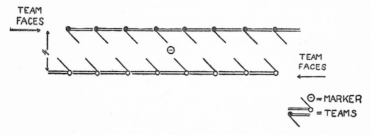

The leader places a volleyball or basketball on the center marker. When he says "Row!"—pronounced as in row a boat—the players on each team who are closest to the ball begin to drive the ball *along the ground,* down the row between the teams, toward the end of the line and in the direction in which his team is facing. Only the right hand must be used and the ball must not be struck or pushed higher than floor level, except to pass over the hands of the players on the rival teams. When the game is played well, every player has a chance to push or strike the ball in order to help it on its way.

When the leader who acts as referee sees that the ball has been lofted over the hand or arm of a player who has not had the chance to touch it, he calls "Hold!" and stops the game and places the ball back in the lane at the point from which it was lofted. The team which first drives the ball to the end of the row which it faces scores goal and is declared winner of that round.

This exciting game requires some strength and some skill.

The player who may not have sufficient strength to force his opponent's hand back can maneuver the ball so that it passes either close to himself or his opponent, thus avoiding direct pressure on the ball. The team which first scores 3 goals is declared winner.

For a change and to exercise the players' left arms and to make the game a little harder, the positions of the teams may be reversed so that they are striking the ball with their left hands instead of their right hands. The lane is, of course, still between the rival teams and the only change in the game is that of the position of the players.

MY BOY!

FOR GIRLS	6 TO 16 PLAYERS	PLAYED INDOORS
JR. HIGH—SR. HIGH	INDIVIDUAL	OR OUTDOORS

The number of participants in this game is limited to the number of round-ended pairs of scissors that the leader of the games can gather in.

A volunteer male of eligible age, who does not know what he is in for, plays the role of the "boy" in this race. Volunteers may be encouraged by the leader asking for a perfect specimen of boyhood or budding manhood for the central figure in this contest. The leader tucks one end of a 16-foot length of paper streamer 2 inches wide under the volunteer's belt. One streamer for each girl competing is required and fastened in the same way. The streamers should be tucked in securely so that they will not pull out easily. The free end of each streamer is given to a girl who stands the full length of it away from the boy who is attached to the other end. Each girl clutches a pair of scissors.

On the word "Go!" each girl begins to cut her streamer carefully down the middle, lengthwise, along its full length so as to reach the victim at the other end as speedily as possible. Any girl who cuts through her streamer crosswise is out of the running. The winner gets her boy—with his consent, of course—as the prize. In the case of a tie, the runners-up may

compete again, holding the scissors in the left hand while
cutting the streamer.

MY GIRL!

This event is played in exactly the same way as the game
above, with a girl victim.

HONEY POTS

FOR BOYS AND GIRLS	8 TO 14 PLAYERS	PLAYED OUTDOORS
ELEMENTARY—SR. HIGH	INDIVIDUAL	OR INDOORS

This is a favorite game for players of all ages in Great
Britain. Grownups, too, find amusement in Honey Pots. The
leader of the games is the owner of the honey and two of the
larger players are prospective buyers. The rest of the players
represent pots of honey and they must not laugh or even
smile during the game. In this game, as in most other games,
a large group of players can be divided into two or more
playing groups, each group playing independently.

The players who are honey pots squat down. They may
balance themselves by touching the ground with their fingers
or hands. The owner of the honey brings the buyers to take
a look at the honey and judge its quality. The buyers push
down lightly on the head and shoulders of different honey
pots and make amusing remarks about the probable quality
of the honey. "This honey is too sweet!" or "Too thick!" or
"Too thin!" a buyer complains. "How would you like to spread
this honey on your bread?" one buyer asks another. "I'm afraid
that it would run off onto my lap!" the other buyer comments.
The honey pots, including the one which is being spoken
about, must not smile.

If the buyers decide to buy one of the pots of honey, they
say, "We'll take this one." When the honey pot spoken of
hears this, it must clasp its hands tightly around its legs just
above the ankles, keeping its elbows stiffly at its sides. The
two buyers each take an elbow with one hand, if the honey

pot is not too heavy, and carry it about 6 paces away. Provided the honey pot does not smile and does not lose its hold on its ankles while being transported, the owner and the buyers are well pleased and the deal goes through. Should the honey pot smile, lose the ankle grip, or hold its arms in such a way that it is too clumsy to carry fairly easily, that honey pot is not purchased and may be the subject of a few disparaging remarks on the part of the owner and would-be buyers.

SACK BALL

FOR BOYS AND GIRLS   10 PLAYERS   PLAYED OUTDOORS
ELEMENTARY—SR. HIGH   TEAM

The gear required for this amusing game is a volleyball or basketball and five white paper-plate markers 6 inches in diameter, with five staples to hold them in place. The ground should be smooth, preferably grassy, and inspected in advance.

A paper plate stapled to the ground marks the center of the field and the kickoff point. A goal 6 feet wide is marked by two paper plates directly opposite the kickoff plate and 20 feet distant. Another goal of the same width is marked directly opposite the first goal and at the same distance from the kickoff plate—20 feet.

There are five players on each team and they wear clean potato sacks, as though competing in a sack race. The sacks must be held up high on the body with *both* hands during the entire game. Any player who intentionally releases his hold on the sack during play is ruled out of the game.

The captain of each team arranges his players in any formation he chooses, though a goalkeeper and at least one back and two forwards are suggested. After the team captains have placed their teams in position, the games leader who referees throws up the ball above the kickoff plate, and the fun is on. Each player tries to kick or drive the ball toward the opponent's goal, using only feet, or legs when the ball is not on the ground. The hands must not be used except for holding up the sack and helping the players to rise from the ground after falls. When a goal is scored by either team, the ball is taken by the referee back to the kickoff plate and the game starts again from that point.

Few rules are required and a little mild shouldering adds to the fun and need not be considered a foul. The game may continue for five or ten minutes or until 2 or 3 goals have been scored by a team. The team scoring the most goals is, of course, the winner.

The players who force their toes into the two front corners of the sack will be able to move faster and with fewer spills than those who don't.

CATCH HANDICAP

FOR BOYS AND GIRLS	4 TO 16 PLAYERS	PLAYED OUTDOORS
ELEMENTARY—SR. HIGH	INDIVIDUAL	OR INDOORS

This is one of a series of Catch Games which can be made quite easy or progressively difficult, to suit the skill of the catchers. All that is needed in the way of equipment is from one to four volleyballs or tennis balls, which are distributed by the leader.

The group stands in a large circle. The player who leads the catching stands in the middle of the circle, while the three or more players who are going to copy his catches also stand, several feet apart, inside the circle. The player who leads then throws his ball into the air and performs some stunt before catching it as it falls. The more difficult the stunt, the harder the game becomes. Players who fail to make any one of the stunt catches drop out of the game. When the player leading the game misses a catch, he is replaced by another catcher who is chosen by the leader.

The leader should suggest at the beginning of the game that some easy catching stunts be done first, such as turning completely around once, clapping the hands twice, touching the knees, touching both elbows, and so on, before catching the falling ball. The difficulty of the pre-catch motions can be gradually increased until the player who sets the catch patterns is kneeling down to catch the ball, spinning around twice or oftener, touching the forehead with both hands stretched up between the legs, and performing other difficult stunts.

Different types of catches will sometimes be decided by whether the balls used are volleyballs or tennis balls.

THROW, TURN AND SIT

FOR BOYS AND GIRLS	12 TO 30 PLAYERS	PLAYED OUTDOORS
ELEMENTARY—JR. HIGH	TEAM	OR INDOORS

From three to ten players stand in line, one behind the other and 2 or 3 feet apart. The players all face a paper-plate marker 15 to 20 feet away and directly in front of the first player in the line. When two or more teams are competing there should be a distance of about 4 feet between teams, and the same number of players on each team.

A leader, holding a volleyball or lightweight basketball, stands just behind a marker, facing one team of players. A leader or thrower is needed for each line of players. When the leader of the games calls "Throw!" each thrower throws the ball to the first player in his line. That player must catch the ball and throw it back as quickly as possible. He then turns completely around and squats where he stood while catching the ball. The leader only throws the ball to the

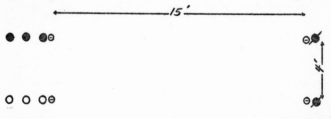

⊖ = MARKERS
8 = PLAYERS
∅ = LEADERS

second player after the first player is squatting on the ground, facing the thrower. The line with all of its players squatting in the correct position first is the winner, provided all of the players have made clean catches.

HOOPLA!

FOR BOYS AND GIRLS	8 TO 20 PLAYERS	PLAYED OUTDOORS
ELEMENTARY—JR. HIGH	INDIVID.—TEAM	OR INDOORS

This simple round-the-circle race game was devised in various forms for use at picnics or any outdoor games tournament. It invariably causes amusement when a girl and boy meet at one of the "hoops," which, sooner or later, is bound to happen.

To play the game, two tennis balls or rubber balls of about the same size, or even two volleyballs, a paper-plate marker 6 inches in diameter, and the hoops formed by the players provide all of the equipment required. All of the players except two form in a big circle. There should be 1 long pace between players and all players should face in the same direction. When the game is about to start, each player raises his arms directly above his head and clasps his fingers so that his arms form a big hoop. A white paper-plate marker is placed between two players in any part of the circle as a starting point. The two players left out of the circle when it was formed now stand inside it, both of them directly alongside the starting marker but facing in opposite directions.

The leader gives each player a ball of the same size. On the word "Go!" each player begins at the starting marker and runs around the circle, passing the ball from hand to hand so that it goes through each hoop. This ball-through-hoop motion continues until the starting marker is reached again. The first player to reach the marker after correctly circling the circle is the winner.

Should the two players reach the same hoop during the race around the circle, it will only add to the difficulty of the race and cause more fun. A player who drops the ball during such an encounter must go back two hoops as a forfeit before continuing around the circle. There should be no pushing of hands or arms to cause intentional interference on the part of either player, however.

No harm can come from a collision on the part of the two players who are circling the circle, as their speed, on account of passing the balls through the hoops, is negligible. Should the leader wish, however, he can have one of the runners make the round from outside the circle while the other player runs around inside the circle. As the runner inside the circle has a slight distance less to run than the player on the outside track, the race should be carried out a second time, with the players changing places for the second round.

This game makes a good relay race, with two teams of equal size. Each team fills one half of the circle and the players on each team touch each other off just as soon as they complete the circle run. The leader who is refereeing the game must be on the lookout as the contesting players meet at various parts of the circle, and he must also see that all of the players in the circle who are forming the hoops do not show preference for their team by, for instance, changing the shapes of their hoops from very round to very oval!

WEAVE THE CIRCLE RELAY

FOR BOYS AND GIRLS   12 TO 20 PLAYERS   PLAYED OUTDOORS
ELEMENTARY—SR. HIGH   TEAM—INDIVID.   OR INDOORS

An even number of players stand in a circle facing inward with 3 feet between players. A white paper-plate marker is stapled to the ground between but 3 feet outside any two players in the circle. These players are each given the Number 1 and the other players are numbered from 2 onward, clockwise on half of the circle and counterclockwise on the other half of the circle.

When the leader calls "Go!" the Number 1 players weave their way on the run, each running in opposite directions, between the players, all the way around the circle, as shown in the diagram. The arrival of the Number 1 player back in place touches off player Number 2, and the relay continues until every player on both teams has circled the circle.

A player who starts too soon, before the number ahead of him is actually back in place, is stopped for a moment by the leader as a penalty. If two or three overeager players on a team start too soon, that team may be considered to have lost

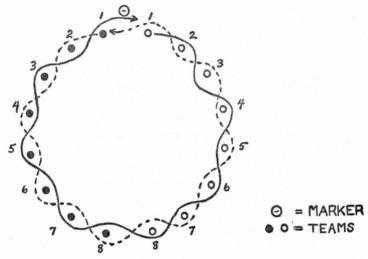

Θ = MARKER
● O = TEAMS

the race by default. The winning team is the one whose players finish correctly first. The winning team may also be decided by the one having top score in two out of three tries. This is a game which develops ability in dodging and teaches the players to be wary as they approach the likely spot where they have to pass members of the rival team. While the speed of the players is broken very considerably by constant circling, making possible collisions a matter of fun rather than hurt, leaders may carry out this relay in two circles, laid out as in the game which follows—Dizzy Circle Relay—should they so wish.

In the individual version of Weave the Circle Relay, each player on a team races the same number in the rival team. In the pause between each race the leader can place the starting marker beside the next pair to race.

DIZZY CIRCLE RELAY

FOR BOYS AND GIRLS   12 TO 32 PLAYERS   PLAYED OUTDOORS
ELEMENTARY—SR. HIGH   TEAM

Here is a race worked out especially for this book to meet the universal demand by players of all ages for a game that would make them "dizzy." This one does!

This amusing relay race is best run in two circles of the same size in order to avoid collision between players of rival teams who are in no condition to help themselves. Each team occupies a circle of about 30 feet in diameter and the players stand 1 long pace apart, each player and team facing in the same direction around the circle. The two circles are 4 feet apart. A white paper-plate marker 6 inches in diameter is placed between the two circles in direct line with a player in each circle, as shown in the diagram. This is the starting point for the race in both circles. The team in one circle will run in a clockwise direction, while the team in the other circle will race counterclockwise, as decided by the leader.

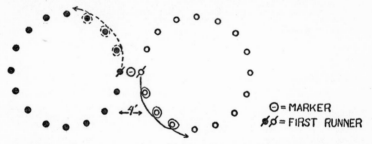

Θ = MARKER
∅∅ = FIRST RUNNER

When the word "Go!" is given, each of the two players opposite the starting mark in each circle runs completely around each of the other players in turn, starting with the player nearest to him. It takes a steady head to accomplish this quickly and correctly, as the player who is doing the circling must not touch any player who is being circled. Most players are forced to slow down considerably or stop for a moment at some part of the circle on the way around. When the first player gets back to his original position, he touches off the second runner, who starts out over the same course. The last player of a team to come in first decides the winning team. Any team that finishes on its feet is a good team whether it is the winner or not!

This relay may also be contested with the runners from each team running in the same direction, though it will not make much difference in the time of the runners.

TURTLES

FOR BOYS	10 TO 20 PLAYERS	PLAYED OUTDOORS
ELEMENTARY—JR. HIGH	TEAM	

Little gear is required for this game; eight paper-plate markers 6 inches in diameter is all. An amusing team game, it is best played by at least two teams with five players on each team. A space of about 40 feet square is marked off for each team by stapling a plate marker to the ground at each corner. Smooth, grassy ground provides a good play area for this game. Each team takes up a spread-out position inside one of the squares. Each group represents four turtles and one keeper.

When the leader calls "Catch!" each turtle keeper tries to tag all of the turtles as quickly as possible. This may seem like an easy job and it would be, were it not for the fact that any turtle in danger of being tagged may avoid capture by dropping to the ground, turning quickly on his back, and raising his arms and legs in the air. He is safe in this position, though he may be tagged getting into it, but a turtle must not remain in it for longer than the slow count of 6, made by the turtle keeper. Should a keeper decide not to chase another turtle when the one he is chasing turns over onto its back, he takes 3 strides away from the upturned turtle, counts 6 slowly and then resumes the chase. The upside-down turtle may take off at any time during the count *but* the keeper cannot go after him until he has finished the count of 6. All turtles touched leave the square as soon as they have been tagged.

A variation of this game is for the keeper to hop on one foot or with both feet together while he is doing the chasing. This gives the turtles more chance and adds more fun to the game.

ZIGZAG BRIDGES

FOR BOYS   12 TO 30 PLAYERS   PLAYED OUTDOORS
ELEMENTARY—JR. HIGH   PARTNER—INDIVID.

This is an amusing game, whether played as an individual or team event. It is best played on a smooth, grassy area. The gear required is two volleyballs or basketballs and a paper-plate marker 6 inches in diameter.

The leader chooses four players to form the first two part-ner-teams. The other players stand in a circle, feet astride, facing toward its center, with an arm's length between players. The marker is stapled to the ground between any two players in the circle. This marks the start and finish point of the race. A partner-team kneels facing each other, one on each side of the marker, one player facing the outside of the circle and the other facing the inside of the circle. The rival team is along-side them at the marker, with the players kneeling in the same positions. Each team is given a ball.

On the word "Go!" each team starts out on all fours to circle the circle, in opposite directions. One partner crawls on the inside of the circle while his partner crawls on the outside of the circle. They drive the ball with one hand only from part-ner to partner, between the astride-position legs of each player, starting with the bridge formed by the nearest player. Of course, the rival teams will meet somewhere on the way around the circle, which adds to the excitement and fun. The only rule is that team members may not touch the ball of the rival team with their hands. Of course, the balls may collide at some point, to the advantage of one of the teams. Immedi-ately the partners of one team reach the starting plate and the ball touches it, they have completed one stage of the game.

Quickly, they kneel side by side and crawl in opposite directions under the astride legs of the players, around the circle, back to the starting marker. Each player must crawl between the legs of the player nearest him, approaching from in front, but returns from behind through the bridge made by the legs of the next player. This zigzag course is continued completely around the circle until the marker plate is reached. There is no denying the fact that passage under the bridges will be congested at times, but often speed and timing will be on the side of the fastest-thinking player. Some patience and courtesy should also be exercised when the paths of the rival teams cross.

It takes a truly alert leader to referee this event, as the methods of progression and the tactics used by rival team members in congested areas require a lot of close watching. Perhaps a leader will be glad to have an assistant to umpire in another part of the circle.

An additional hazard, which makes it hard to guess which team will win, is caused by the rule that *both* partners in a team must be back at the finishing marker in order to decide which is the winning team.

Played as an individual event, two opposing players start out in opposite directions from the starting marker and circle the circle twice, in the same way as the partner-team did, except that they will have to handle the ball on their own, which difficulty merits the privilege of each player using both hands to propel and guide the ball on its rounds. The first player to make the double circle of the circle correctly is the winner.

HOP BALL

FOR BOYS AND GIRLS	4 TO 20 PLAYERS	PLAYED OUTDOORS
ELEMENTARY—JR. HIGH	INDIVID.—TEAM	OR INDOORS

The gear required for this game is a volleyball or a basket-ball for each individual or team and four white paper-plate markers 9 inches in diameter for each team or player. The plate markers for this game can be either placed on or stapled to the ground. The leader puts a marker on the ground at the starting point, then places the other three markers, each 10 feet apart, in a straight line away from it. This forms a row for either an individual player or a team, and there should be a 3-foot lane between the rows of markers.

The leader places a ball 2 feet away from each starting marker and a player stands behind each ball. The players must hop on the right foot only, kicking the balls ahead of them around and close to each marker but without touching any of them. Should a player touch a marker with the ball, he must go back two markers as a forfeit and recommence from there. Upon arrival at the last marker, the player kicks the ball onto it, then kicks it all the way back to the starting marker while hopping only on the left foot. If a player loses balance and has to put either foot on the ground for support, he must hop back three hops, driving the ball before him, and recommence the race from that point.

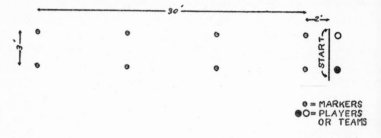

Team play is best carried out in the form of a relay race; two or more teams, each with the same number of players, start with two or more players behind each end of their row of markers. After the first player drives the ball down the line around each marker and onto the fourth marker, while hopping on the right foot, the first player at that end kicks the ball back to the starting marker while hopping only on the left foot. The game continues in this way until all players on a team have had a turn at circling the markers. The last player on a team to complete the course correctly decides the winning team.

With older players, the leader may decide to let all players on each team line up behind the ball at the starting marker and have each player on the team kick the ball down to the fourth marker and back to the starting point, the first hop being made on the right foot and the return on the left foot. Immediately the ball is kicked onto the first marker, the next player on the team takes over.

HOBBLED TWINS FOOTBALL

FOR BOYS   12 TO 16 PLAYERS   PLAYED OUTDOORS
ELEMENTARY—SR. HIGH   TEAM

The only gear needed for this amusing soccer match is a volleyball, basketball, or football and five paper-plate markers 6 inches in diameter. A 3-foot strip of strong cloth 2 or 3 inches wide is also needed for each two players. Since this game is played in three-legged race style, leaders who prefer to fasten the partners together both at the ankles and just below the knees should provide an extra binding, 3 feet longer than that used for the ankle tie, in order to take care of the second tie.

Two goals 8 feet wide are marked about 50 feet apart by stapling two plate markers for each goal, with the staples described in Chapter 3. The ground on which this game is played should be smooth, flat, and, if possible, grassy. The center of the playing field is marked by stapling the fifth plate in the middle of the area halfway between the two goals. There is little point in marking side lines since the three-legged footballers are not likely to get too far afield!

A team of three or four pairs of players takes up any positions decided on by its captain, after a pair of players stand by the center kickoff plate facing the opposing team's goal. The catch in the match is introduced at this point, if the players have not already guessed it from the name of the game, since each pair of players have their ankles tied firmly together as though they were taking part in a three-legged race. The twin-partners will need a great deal of co-ordination, and still more patience, in order to play a decent game of soccer or, in fact, any sort of game at all!

The games leader can referee the game. He places the ball on the kickoff plate and gives the word to kick off when both pairs of players playing center position are ready. From there on, it is anybody's game and anyone's guess as to which team will win. Hands must not be used throughout the game except for balance and push-ups from the ground in case of falls, which will probably keep them occupied. The ball may be kicked with any feet the partners find convenient. Fouls must not be allowed, and the ball must be returned to center after each goal.

TWO TO THREE

FOR BOYS	4 TO 10 PLAYERS	PLAYED OUTDOORS
ELEMENTARY—JR. HIGH	PARTNER	

This amusing game was devised on the spot by the author while directing a Picnic Games Program for players of all ages. The idea came to mind immediately following a request for a Three-Legged Race, and surpassed the rather ancient three-legged event in popularity after its first trial.

The race has nothing to do with the time of day, though it does require skillful timing on the part of the players. Its name refers to the fact that it is a race contested on two hands and practically three knees by each two-man team contesting.

A line is marked on smooth, level, grassy, and inspected ground, with white tape or paper-plate markers stapled in place. Directly opposite it and 30 feet distant, another line is marked. Partners form teams of two and kneel side by side with their fingers touching the starting line. There should be a short space between teams. The player on the left in each team places his right arm over his partner's shoulder and holds it with his right hand. The boy on the right puts his left arm across his partner's shoulders, holding the left shoulder with his left hand.

The leader of the games now securely fastens the partners'

knees and ankles which are nearest each other with 2 or 3 inch wide strips of strong cloth. One tie should cover the ankles and the other one should be fastened just below the knees. The race is now ready to go forward and when the leader says "Go!" the teams set off for the line in front of them. When they reach it they crawl just over it, turn around, and race back to the starting point, where the first team to arrive is declared the winner.

CUP KICK TUG OF WAR

FOR BOYS AND GIRLS   4 TO 12 PLAYERS   PLAYED OUTDOORS
ELEMENTARY—SR. HIGH   INDIVIDUAL   OR INDOORS

Four players stand in a square formation, facing outward. Each holds one corner of a 40-foot length of stout rope, the two ends of which have been tied securely together. Each player should hold the rope with both hands, with hands held above waist level. A large paper cup is placed about 6 feet away from and directly in front of each player.

On the word "Kick!" each player pushes steadily forward

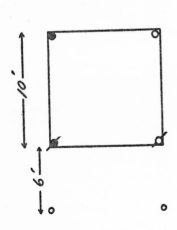

o = CUPS
o o o o= PLAYERS

and tries to kick the cup directly in front of him. The cup must be kicked over to score. Players must not jerk forward nor gather in rope on either side of them. They should hold the rope in the same place throughout the tug and observe the square formation as much as possible. Should the players get too far out of line in the course of the tug, the games leader stops the players and re-forms the square before they start to push again. The first player to kick the cup over is the winner.

6.

Tag Games

PLAYERS all over the world like to vary and complicate Tag Games. They have, since prehistoric times, invented many ways of making the simple chasing and tagging of other players more difficult in certain tag versions. Various "safe" positions for a player in which he cannot be tagged have also been added. In these positions a player is safe, at least until *It* steps back some distance and counts up to 10, after which the chase begins again unless the rules agreed on call for another player to be pursued immediately the one being chased assumes a safe position. A player may be considered safe when he stoops down and touches the ground, or wood, or iron, or other things.

The forms of tag are so many and varied that it is an easy task to record at least fifty different versions. In this chapter the author prefers to describe only eighteen games, a number of which have been devised by him and have not before appeared in print.

INTERFERENCE TAG

FOR BOYS AND GIRLS	4 TO 12 PLAYERS	PLAYED OUTDOORS
ELEMENTARY—JR. HIGH	PARTNER	OR INDOORS

This tag game is played in reverse, with the players trying to tag *It*. To even things up, *It* has a partner who tries to prevent *It* from being tagged by the other players. The partner who runs interference for *It* may not be tagged, but all players tagged by him are out. *It* may not tag the other players and is out of the game after being tagged three times. A new *It* and partner can be chosen for each new game.

ELBOW TAG

FOR BOYS AND GIRLS   4 TO 16 PLAYERS   PLAYED OUTDOORS
ELEMENTARY—JR. HIGH   INDIVIDUAL

In this tag variation the tagger must try to tag another player only on the elbow. It does not count when the player is tagged anywhere else, even on the arm, if the spot tagged is above or below the elbow. The first player who volunteers to be *It* holds his right elbow as he starts the first chase in the game. A player tagged on the elbow becomes the new *It* and must hold the elbow which was tagged when taking up the chase of the other players. In this position his tagging hand is the one on the same side as the elbow which he is holding. If *It* releases the hold on his elbow to tag with the hand which he has freed, it does not count and a player so tagged does not become *It*.

It comes as a considerable relief to the taggers when the leader decides that *It* does not need to hold his elbow while chasing the other players. He may give *It* even a greater break by ruling that those chased and *not It* must hold elbows, with either hand, as they run. This reduces *It's* targets by one, but this handicap is offset to some degree by the fact that he can get around much faster when he is not holding an elbow.

CIRCLE OUT TAG

FOR BOYS AND GIRLS   4 TO 10 PLAYERS   PLAYED INDOORS
ELEMENTARY—JR. HIGH   INDIVIDUAL   OR OUTDOORS

The idea for this game came to the author when he heard a games leader call to a group of tag players, "Circle out!" The circle which he meant had nothing to do with circles on the ground, yet the idea, stirred by his remark, originated Circle Out Tag.

Three circles each 4 feet in diameter are drawn inside a 30-foot triangle, as shown in the diagram. The players stand at any points they wish inside the triangle. *It* starts the chase

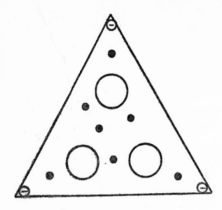

⊖ = MARKERS
● = PLAYERS

from the center of the triangle and all players tagged by him are out of the game.

The added hazard in this fast-moving game is that any player who puts a foot or any part of a foot inside a circle is also out of the game. The game continues until all players have been tagged or ruled out for touching a circle. The last remaining player becomes the new *It*. With more players, and room, a 40-foot triangle can be used.

FLIP FLAP TAG

FOR BOYS AND GIRLS   4 TO 20 PLAYERS   PLAYED OUTDOORS
ELEMENTARY   INDIVIDUAL   OR INDOORS

This tag game is similar to one the author saw Dutch children play which might be roughly translated as "Ducking the Windmill Sails."

The players stand in line, one behind the other, while *It*, the tagger, stands 15 feet away and directly in front of the line of players, with his back to it.

When the leader says "Go!" the tagger immediately begins to move his arms in a stiff position from his sides up to shoulder level or a little above and then down again. The first player moves forward and tries to dodge directly under either of the flailing arms without being tagged. Players must not creep or move outside range of the rising and falling arms, and those who do so are out of the game. As soon as the first player is tagged or manages to get past without being touched, the next player in line advances and the game continues until all of the players have had a chance. The players who get through successfully without being tagged return to the end of the line for another try.

The difficulty for the players who run the gauntlet lies in the fact that the tagger can move both arms or either arm at any reasonable speed he likes and he can increase speed without a moment's notice. An alert tagger may work his arms quite slowly for a moment or two, allowing one or two players to pass under his arms with ease, then suddenly increase the pace so that the next player or two are tagged as they attempt to stoop under and pass. New taggers are chosen by the leader either after all players in one game have been tagged or when the tagger becomes tired.

When there are ten or more players, it is best to have two taggers and form two lines, so that the game moves faster for all of the players.

MONKEY ON A STRING TAG

FOR BOYS AND GIRLS	6 TO 16 PLAYERS	PLAYED OUTDOORS
ELEMENTARY—JR. HIGH	INDIVIDUAL	OR INDOORS

One of the players is a keeper and holds a loop at one end of a length of strong cord or light rope 15 to 20 feet in length. The other end of the rope is fastened to the back of the belt of a player who has volunteered to play the part of the monkey. The monkey stands beside the keeper at the start of the game and the other players circle the keeper and try to touch him or come as close to him as possible without being tagged by the monkey. The keeper cannot tag players who come close and must not move from the original position throughout the game. The monkey chases the players and, by using different ruses and making sudden, unexpected rushes, tags as many of the players as possible.

The game is best played when the leader chooses a new *It* and a new monkey after a monkey has tagged from three to eight players, whereupon the game starts again. This mode of play assures keener competition in dodging the monkey than when the player tagged becomes the monkey.

Another version of this game is to allow both keeper and monkey to chase the other players within a clearly defined area but, as before, only the monkey is allowed to tag the players who come within tagging range.

CIRCUMVENT TAG

FOR BOYS AND GIRLS	4 TO 20 PLAYERS	PLAYED OUTDOORS
ELEMENTARY—SR. HIGH	INDIVIDUAL	OR INDOORS

Running circles around someone pays off in this rather strenuous tag game. *It* gives the other players about a 20-foot start and then sets out to tag any one of them. The player who is being chased can escape from *It* by running entirely around him, once. Good sportsmanship dictates that this be done at as close quarters to *It* as is reasonably safe. Naturally, *It* tries to thwart encirclement by a ruse, such as running as closely alongside the boy he is chasing as that player, who fears being tagged, will let him. A player can also escape being tagged by outrunning *It* without attempting to circle him, but this is not sporting. *It* may tag from one to three players in succession before the leader chooses a new tagger.

This is an exciting and amusing game where dodging and sudden stops both on the part of the hunter and hunted can get good results.

As in all similar tag games, some sort of reasonably restricted boundaries must be strictly observed to assure good sport and good fun.

BALL OUT TAG

FOR BOYS AND GIRLS   4 TO 20 PLAYERS   PLAYED OUTDOORS
ELEMENTARY—JR. HIGH   INDIVID.—TEAM

It stands inside a circle 20 feet in diameter and holds a volleyball or a large, soft rubber ball. The other players gather all around the circle, getting as close to *It* as they dare. *It* knocks the ball out of the circle with his open hand and then rushes out of the circle to tag as many players as he can. Those tagged are out of the game. As the ball is being knocked out of the circle, the players try to catch or intercept it, without entering inside the circle, in order to put it back in the circle again, because *It* cannot tag anyone while the ball is within the circle, nor can he tag a player with the ball when that player is taking it back to the circle.

In this, as in all other tag games of its sort, boundaries must be clearly understood or marked in order to get the most out of the game.

Once *It* has knocked the ball outside the circle, he continues to chase and tag as many players as possible, while awaiting the arrival of the unhappy moment when a blast of the leader's whistle tells that the ball has been put inside the circle. *It* must then rush back to bang the ball out again before he can do any more tagging. The game continues until all of the players have been tagged or until *It* becomes too tired to carry on, is replaced, and the game started again.

Two teams of equal size can compete in this game, and the one which manages to tag all of the players on the other side in the shortest time is the winner.

PILLAR TAG

FOR BOYS AND GIRLS   10 TO 30 PLAYERS   PLAYED OUTDOORS
ELEMENTARY—JR. HIGH   INDIVIDUAL   OR INDOORS

The leader marks a circle 30 feet in diameter on the ground. Four players, who play the part of pillars for the first game, stand motionless inside the circle in the places marked on the diagram. Two taggers also stand inside the circle, but they can move about within the circle as they please. The other players stand around and just outside the circle marked on the ground.

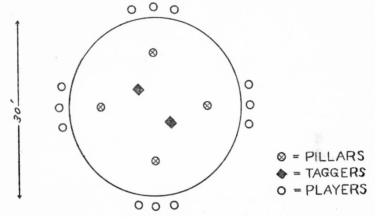

⊗ = PILLARS
◆ = TAGGERS
O = PLAYERS

On the word "Go!" four players named by the leader, one from each side of the circle, rush or move slowly into the circle. Each tries to run completely around the pillar nearest to him without being tagged by one of the taggers. All players tagged inside the circle before they have reached and circled a pillar are out of the game, as are those who run out of the circle to escape being tagged. All players who succeed in circling a pillar without being tagged report to the leader and get the choice of being either a tagger or pillar, or of playing from outside of the circle, as before, in the next game. As soon as the first four players have made their try, the leader names the next four players, one from each side of the circle as before, to make the pillar-circling attempt.

It will be seen that the choosing of four players for each round and the assignment of a different pillar to each of the four players is to avoid possibility of collision between the players. The author devised the above method of playing this game and the special pillar assignment arrangement after watching the game played in England on a free-for-all basis, with all players outside the circle contesting simultaneously —with rather devastating results!

TURNABOUT TAG

FOR BOYS AND GIRLS　　　6 TO 20 PLAYERS　　　PLAYED OUTDOORS
ELEMENTARY—JR. HIGH　　　INDIVIDUAL　　　OR INDOORS

The players start out in a straight horizontal line from a base line which is marked on the ground, with *It* walking about 3 short paces ahead of them.

The *turnabout* comes when *It* suddenly and unexpectedly whirls around, chases, and tags as many players as possible before they can get safely back across the base line, where they are safe. Those tagged are out of the game. The game continues until all players have been tagged. A new *It* then volunteers or is chosen and the game starts again.

The excitement in this game is caused by the uncertainty of *It's* movements and ruses. *It* should at all times while advancing walk in front of the line but he should veer from the middle of the line toward either end of it, still keeping a distance of about 3 feet between himself and the part of the line of players that he walks in front of. In this way he is closer to different groups of players as the game progresses. *It* can cause panic and amusement by merely swinging his head and arms around suddenly, while continuing to advance. Many of the players make a panicky and needless rush for the safety of the base line when *It* pretends to turn from time to time. However, doing it too often spoils the effect. *It* often has to wait for the line to re-form, after one of his pretended turns, before continuing the game. If so many players break out of line when *It* stages a ruse that the forward advance is slowed down too much, the leader may rule all players out of the game who actually turn and run simply because *It* feints. *It's* head and body movements can also be used as strategy to conceal the actual moment of his unexpected charge toward the players.

Another version of this game is for *It* to advance as before but in different ways, such as hopping, jumping with both feet together, crawling a short distance, and so forth, while the other players must follow him in exactly the same manner. *It* may deceive the other players still more easily in this form of the game, catching them off guard by pretending to drop on all fours, after he has actually done so once or twice in the course of a game, and swinging around and giving chase instead.

DOUBLE CROSS TAG

FOR BOYS AND GIRLS   4 TO 20 PLAYERS   PLAYED OUTDOORS
ELEMENTARY—JR. HIGH   INDIVIDUAL

Because one player remarked to another while playing ordinary Cross Tag, "You tried to double-cross me!" the author devised Double Cross Tag.

This variation of Cross Tag may be introduced into any tag game when at least four players take part. When any two players manage to cross at the same time between the player being chased and *It*, the tagger must stop chasing the player he is after and chase either one of the two players who crossed between him and his quarry. This form of tag gives a slow runner a chance of escape and it also gives the tagger a chance, since players often cross when there is hardly a sporting chance of doing so safely.

AFRICAN TAG

FOR BOYS AND GIRLS   3 TO 10 PLAYERS   PLAYED OUTDOORS
ELEMENTARY—JR. HIGH   INDIVIDUAL

The natives of some West African tribes "rest" by placing the arch of one foot just above the knee of the other leg. They find this so restful a position that they frequently stand that way for hours at a time. This habit gave the author an idea for this tag game.

The player who is being hotly pursued by *It* can save himself by stopping suddenly, if he can, and standing on one leg. This sounds easy, but it is the sudden stop while running and maintaining balance that adds one difficulty, while the second one is the fact that a certain leg position is required for this form of tag. While the player being chased is momentarily safe just as soon as he lifts a foot from the ground, he must place that foot in a special position, while *It* watches, before he is really safe. Yes, the position is the one dear to the heart of some African natives. A foot, either one, must be placed so that the arch rests just above the knee of the other leg, and this position must be held while *It* counts slowly to 6. If the player does not put both feet on the ground before *It* has counted to 6, then *It* must go after another player; but if the player loses balance and puts both feet on the ground, he becomes *It*.

RELAY TAG

FOR BOYS AND GIRLS   6 TO 16 PLAYERS   PLAYED OUTDOORS
ELEMENTARY—JR. HIGH   INDIVIDUAL

A volunteer *It* chases a player who is carrying a tightly rolled newspaper. The player pursued escapes by passing the rolled newspaper to the player who is nearest to him. That player must immediately accept the roll when it is offered to him. *It* must always chase the player who is carrying the roll. The player who is tagged while carrying it becomes *It*.

Clearly marked or understood boundaries should be observed in this game, as in nearly all other tag games, in order to make it more sporting and give *It* a chance.

While a short wooden stick can replace the rolled newspaper it is not suggested as a good substitute, for a player may get poked with it during the heat of the game. The rolled newspaper can be given more permanent form by tightly rolling a standard-size newspaper into a roll about 12 inches long and 1 or 1½ inches in diameter and then binding it firmly together with tough string, and it can be made even more lasting by covering it with a piece of thick cloth which is kept in place by winding twine around it.

SWISS TAG

FOR BOYS AND GIRLS   2 TO 10 PLAYERS   PLAYED OUTDOORS
ELEMENTARY—JR. HIGH   INDIVIDUAL   OR INDOORS

This form of tag, played by only two players at a time, is based on the way Swiss skiers race around markers.

Eight or more paper-plate markers 6 inches in diameter are laid on the ground in any zigzag pattern, with a distance of about 6 feet separating markers. The player who is *It* must follow the player who is to be tagged, over exactly the same

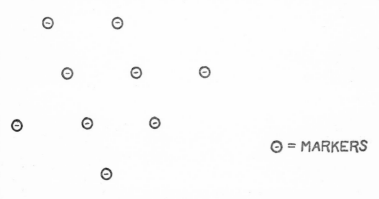

⊖ = MARKERS

course. The player who is being chased must run completely around each marker but he may double in and out around the markers, circling any ones that he chooses, in order to make it difficult for *It*. A games leader may rule that any player, including *It*, who displaces two markers in succession is out of the game.

The markers may be arranged in different patterns from time to time, and skillful arragement of them makes this an exciting form of tag.

BALANCE TAG

FOR BOYS AND GIRLS   2 TO 20 PLAYERS   PLAYED OUTDOORS
ELEMENTARY—JR. HIGH   INDIVIDUAL   OR INDOORS

The players stand in pairs facing each other with their arms stretched forward just below shoulder level, so that only their finger tips touch. There should be about 2 feet between the pairs of players in line. The two players directly facing each other are rivals, and when the leader says "Go!" they try to tag each other anywhere above the wrist of the extended hands. The players must not move their feet during the contest. Each player spars for an opening and tries to entice his rival to lean forward so that he may be tagged. A player may also try to throw his rival off balance by slapping or pushing the extended hand. The player who tags his opponent most often in a contest of from three to six rounds is the winner. This game helps to develop balance, alertness, and quickness of movement.

ARM FOLD TAG

FOR BOYS AND GIRLS   2 TO 14 PLAYERS   PLAYED OUTDOORS
ELEMENTARY—JR. HIGH   INDIVIDUAL

In this form of tag the players are handicapped instead of *It*. All players except the tagger run with their arms folded across their chests in this version of the game. The players should be warned by the leader to unfold their arms instantly if they stumble or seem about to fall, though most players will invariably do so instinctively without being cautioned. More players will have an opportunity to become *It* in a shorter time in Arm Fold Tag and many of them will develop new skills in dodging while playing this tag version.

FROG TAG

FOR BOYS AND GIRLS   2 TO 12 PLAYERS   PLAYED OUTDOORS
ELEMENTARY—JR. HIGH   INDIVIDUAL   OR INDOORS

All players, including *It,* must hop in this game. During the first few minutes of play all players hop on the right foot. In the second part they hop on the left foot. The times are fixed by the leader; and the third part of the game will cause laughs and some spills on the grass because the players hop on both feet, with legs held close together and ankles touching. All tagging and dodging is done in this position. The temptation to break into the usual run, or hop on one foot only, is great, but players who do so are ruled out of the game by the leader.

The most exciting way for older players to enjoy this game of tag is to play the double frog-hop way, with their ankles tied closely together with a yard long strip of soft, strong cloth 3 or 4 inches wide. This will go twice or three times around the ankles, and when it is really tight the two ends are tied in front with a square knot. This is the best knot to use and it is one which will save a great deal of time and bother when the ankle ties have to be taken off.

BALL TAG

FOR BOYS AND GIRLS   4 TO 14 PLAYERS   PLAYED OUTDOORS
ELEMENTARY—JR. HIGH   INDIVIDUAL

This game calls for a limited and defined play area even more than other forms of tag games. All games of tag should have a clearly specified and not too large area in which they are played, in order to prevent the game from becoming a lengthy chase of one player while the others are left far behind and virtually out of the game.

Ball Tag is played with a large or small, soft rubber ball, or even a volleyball which is not fully inflated. Large balls are actually best, as they cannot be thrown so far and much less time is lost in retrieving them after a miss. *It* counts to 6 while the other players scatter in all directions. He then chases the players and tries to hit one of them below shoulder level with the ball. When a player is hit with the ball, below shoulder level only, he becomes the new *It* and the game continues. Players will find it much better fun to dodge and duck and twist to avoid being hit, rather than run away fast in a straight line. Daring the tagger at fairly close quarters and trusting to quick footwork to escape being hit is the most sporting way to play, and it also provides the most excitement and fun.

MONKEY TAG

FOR BOYS AND GIRLS   4 TO 12 PLAYERS   PLAYED OUTDOORS
ELEMENTARY—JR. HIGH   INDIVIDUAL

This is a strenuous form of tag, best played on a small grassy area. *It* and all players must move with hands—or finger tips at least—and feet touching the ground, except when *It* raises a hand to tag a player. This is a good game to work off steam but it should only be played for a brief period of time.

A variation is for all players to move on hands and knees only.

7.

Novelty Games

GUESS!

FOR BOYS AND GIRLS   2 TO 12 PLAYERS   PLAYED INDOORS
JR. HIGH—SR. HIGH   INDIVIDUAL   OR OUTDOORS

Both this game and Guessing Unlimited, which follows, were developed from a somewhat similar game which the author saw children play in London's Hyde Park. The players called their game "Guess Up and Down." It was played on a flight of steps, but that needless hazard has been removed without the games suffering in consequence.

These games had their first tryouts in universities, colleges, and high schools in the American and Canadian Northwest. Their popularity was such that frequently college girls from the University of Vancouver met and thanked the author on the street and in buses for introducing the games. It appeared that when the girls outthought and outguessed the boys at Guess! the boys gave the winners candy or soft drinks. The author was told by a college student in Los Angeles that the dean of a college in that area vowed to shoot the instigator of the game, which left its traces in the form of chalk lines on the walks, halls, and dormitory floors of his college.

This exciting game is best played with four players contesting at once, using two sets of markers as shown in the diagram. The drawing shows how the strips of paper or cardboard, representing steps, are placed on the ground. Colored strips—white for the steps, blue for the starting strips, and red for the winning strip—make a pattern which is easily understood by the players. Chalk may be used to mark the

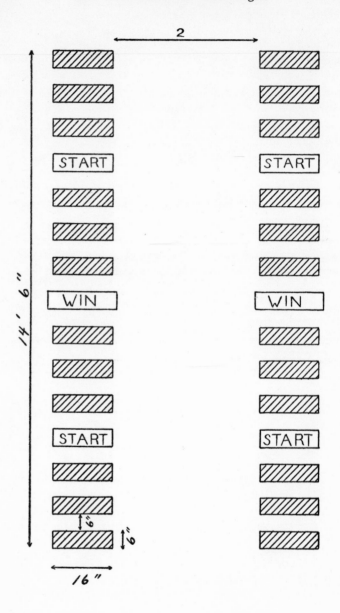

pattern on the ground instead of paper. Twelve white markers, two blue markers, and one red marker are required for each two players. The two players in each line stand on strips marked *Start,* and each player is given an ordinary marble. The players keep their hands behind their backs with a marble in one of them. The two players try to outguess and outwit each other in this way. Either player is given the first guess. The other player then brings his hands around in front of his body with the marble in one of them. The guesser calls out "Right" or "Left." The player who is not guessing opens his hands to prove the guess right or wrong. If the guesser is correct he goes *forward* onto the next strip, but when the guess is wrong he goes *back* one strip. *Only* the player who has guessed moves.

In this form of the game, players take turns at guessing, whether a guess is right or wrong. The game continues until one player reaches the winning red strip, or until one player has been outguessed off the last strip and out of the game. This leaves the last remaining player a winner, no matter on which strip he may be when his opponent is forced off and out.

GUESSING UNLIMITED

FOR BOYS AND GIRLS	2 TO 12 PLAYERS	PLAYED INDOORS
JR. HIGH—SR. HIGH	INDIVIDUAL	OR OUTDOORS

This game is played on the step-strips arranged as in the preceding game of Guess! The difference is that the guesser may guess again and again, as long as he guesses correctly each time. By correct and exceptional guessing he may work from the starting strip to the step next to the winning strip, at which point a wrong guess may start him on his way back to the starting strip, or beyond, as the new guesser takes over.

A player in this game—as in Guess!—tries to outsmart as well as outguess the other player. The player extending his hands tries to outwit the guesser by looking at the hand which does not hold the marble and clutching that hand more tightly than the other. Some players can actually tell which hand holds the marble by looking into the holder's eyes!

When one player is not actually forced out of the game for lack of steps, the winner can be decided at almost any point in the game by a glance at their positions on the strips at that particular moment.

LADY ANNE

FOR GIRLS	6 TO 18 PLAYERS	PLAYED INDOORS
ELEMENTARY—JR. HIGH	INDIVIDUAL	OR OUTDOORS

This game has long been a favorite with girls in England. There are several versions. The one which follows was devised by the author.

The players sit in a circle. One of them holds a small rubber ball, not larger than a tennis ball.

The leader takes one of the players just outside the circle and has her close her eyes while the other players pass the ball from hand to hand in any direction. The leader either points to the girl who should hide the ball on her lap or the players may decide for themselves. The girl with the ball covers it carefully with her hands while the other players pretend to conceal balls on their laps.

When the ball is hidden, the leader asks the girl outside the circle to open her eyes and go into the middle of the circle. She does so and looks carefully at the hands and face of each player, trying to decide which one holds the hidden ball. When she has made up her mind she recites:

> My lady Anne sits in the sun,
> Fair as a lily, brown as a bun;
> She sends her greetings to one and all
> And asks *you,* please, to throw me the ball.

When the guesser says *you,* she points directly at the player whom she believes holds the hidden ball.

If the girl pointed to has the ball, she must throw it to the girl in the center of the circle and becomes the next guesser.

If the guesser has guessed wrongly she tries again. Should she not guess correctly in three tries, the leader or the players choose another girl to take her place and the game begins again.

The introduction of a second, and even a third, ball into the game by the leader, when there are more than ten players, makes the game a little easier for the girl who is guessing and gives more than one player the fun of hiding a ball.

SAM THE SLEUTH

FOR BOYS	6 TO 18 PLAYERS	PLAYED INDOORS
ELEMENTARY—JR. HIGH	INDIVIDUAL	OR OUTDOORS

This is an observation game which has been devised for boys, because the girls have a special detecting game of their own in this book, called Lady Anne.

The only equipment required is a tennis ball or any ball of about the same size. The use of a smaller ball makes the game harder for the "detective." When there is a group of more than ten players the game may be made easier by the leader introducing a second ball into the game. This version makes the work of deduction less hard for the detective, as two players, instead of only one, provide an extra chance to guess correctly.

The boys sit in a circle or semicircle and the leader chooses one to be the detective. While he stands outside the circle with his eyes covered, the leader gives out the number of balls to be used in the game. The players pass the balls from hand to hand until they are hidden. Each ball is covered by two hands resting on the lap. When there are two balls, each one must be hidden by a different player. The fact that all of the players will hold their hands as though they are hiding the ball, even though they don't, does not make the game easier for the amateur sleuth.

When the balls are hidden, the leader tells the sleuth to open his eyes and go into the circle. When he gets there, he takes a good look around at the hands and *faces* of the players before saying anything. Then he says, still staring hard at the players:

> Sam the Sleuth has his eyes on you all
> And says, yes, *you* there, throw me the ball.

When Sam says *you*, he points directly to the player who he thinks has the ball. Should Sam guess correctly, the leader chooses a new sleuth. If the would-be detective makes a wrong guess the first time, he takes two more turns at guessing, unless he guesses correctly on the second try.

SLALOM

FOR BOYS AND GIRLS   2 TO 16 PLAYERS   PLAYED OUTDOORS
ELEMENTARY—JR. HIGH   INDIVID.—TEAM   OR INDOORS

This game came into being as the author watched Swiss skiers weave around marker flags in the course of a popular *slalom* race. Thinking it would prove difficult to even run around markers in a race against time or other racers, the game was developed to prove the thought right, or wrong. You will find that it was right!

In this snowless version of a ski race, players race around six or more markers placed on the ground. The diagram shows how these markers are arranged. Although the markers should be placed 4 feet apart when playing outdoors, the distance may be reduced to 2½ feet when playing indoors or where space is limited. Each player has his own line of markers, made of paper saucers 5 inches in diameter. Each set of markers can be painted in a bright and different show-card color.

On the word "Go!" each player races from the first to the end marker, following the path around each marker indicated in the drawing. The racers should be ready to sit down just as soon as they feel giddy. The first player to finish, provided he has circled the markers correctly, is the winner.

To make the race harder for older players, the race may be run from the starting point, around the end marker, and back

SLALOM

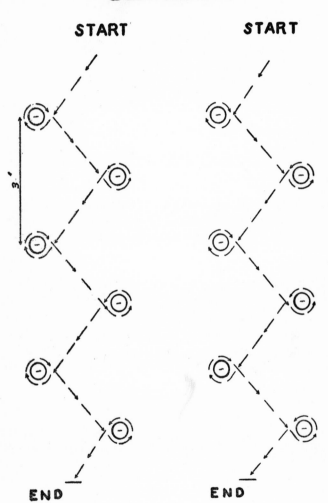

to the starting point. The return trip is made in the opposite direction from that indicated by the arrows in the drawing. Additional markers can also be added to lengthen the race.

When teams of three or four players race over each course, one-way or round-trip, the players on each team stand one behind the other behind the starting marker, completing the course one at a time when touched off by the runner ahead of them.

KNOTTY

FOR BOYS AND GIRLS　　　　2 TO 12 PLAYERS　　　　PLAYED INDOORS
ELEMENTARY—JR. HIGH　　　INDIVID.—TEAM　　　　OR OUTDOORS

This game is sometimes played by the Indian children of the Pueblos. Knots and Pueblo-made cord are associated with them since the time that some of the Pueblo people started to keep track of the arrival of important events by undoing knots from a length of cord, one knot being undone for each passing sun.

Two lengths of heavy cord or rope, 18 inches long, are all that is required for this guessing game when only two players or two teams are competing. A length of cord is given to each two players or teams. The players sit facing each other. One player holds the cords behind his back and makes from one to four knots in it. He also may make none if he likes. When he has made the number of knots he wishes, he still holds the the cord behind his back with the left hand and holds his right hand out in front of him, as a sign that he is ready. The other player, or one player on the rival team, now guesses how many knots are on the cord. After the guess has been made, the player who made the knots brings the cord from behind his back and holds it out in front of him, with his left hand. Points are scored for the player or team guessing correctly, and then the other player or team gets a chance to do the knot making. Of course, the player who makes the knots may pretend that he is working hard to make four knots, while in reality he is making none, or only one.

The leader should not allow a player more than a few moments to make the simple single knots, nor the guessing side more than a few moments to decide how many knots have been made. If these points are not observed, the game is slowed down considerably.

As a variation of this game, the player or team which guesses correctly the number of knots is allowed to continue to guess until they guess wrong; then it is the turn of the other player or team to do the guessing.

TAP TRAP

FOR BOYS AND GIRLS	6 TO 20 PLAYERS	PLAYED INDOORS
ELEMENTARY—JR. HIGH	INDIVIDUAL	OR OUTDOORS

This is an excellent game to develop alertness and self-control in the players—traits that will serve them well while playing other games in which they have to keep their wits about them.

A stool, wooden chair, or upended box is placed in the middle of an 8-foot circle marked on the ground, and a circle 30 feet in diameter surrounds the smaller circle. The players form a close circle, facing inward, around the edge of the 8-foot circle. The leader stands beside the stool, holding a short hardwood stick in one hand. He tells the players that immediately after he has tapped the stool three times he will drop the stick and tag as many players as possible before they can reach safety just outside the big circle. The leader will not chase beyond its edge. All players tagged are out of the game. The last few remaining players, after half a dozen chases by the leader, may be counted as joint winners, or the game may go on until every player has been tagged. There is another hazard which rules players out of this game. Any player who begins to run before the third tap has actually been given is out of the game. This is a tricky feature of the game, since many players are tempted to run on the second beat, if not the first, so that they may have a good start in case there is a third tap followed by the chase.

The leader adds excitement and suspense to the fun by varying the number of beats, striking one tap after two taps, then two again, before striking the three taps needed to herald the chase. It is unfair for a leader to pause slightly prior to giving the third tap, when three taps is the number he has decided to give. Such uneven tapping rightly gives the players the impression that the leader has tapped twice, then once, and they will not run. To vary the method and difficulty of play, the leader may ask the players to face him before the first three taps, turn their backs to him for the next series, or several series, of taps, and so on. Older players may take turns at tapping out the signals.

To add further hazards to this already hazardous game, the players may be asked to raise their left hand above their heads for one tap and the right hand for two taps. Those older players who do the wrong thing may be ruled out of the game. This arm-raising distraction also disconcerts the players so that often when the three taps sound, they stand like rabbits in a flashlight beam instead of high-tailing it to avoid being tagged.

HAZARD

FOR BOYS AND GIRLS   8 TO 20 PLAYERS   PLAYED OUTDOORS
ELEMENTARY—JR. HIGH   INDIVIDUAL   OR INDOORS

Six big, cone-shaped paper cups are placed in a circle with a distance of 3 or 4 feet between cups. The cups are painted with show-card or other paints in the following colors: one cup is red, one blue, one white, one yellow, and two black. The cups are placed in a circle with the two black cups on opposite sides of the ring. The cups score in this way: red, 3 points; blue, 2 points; white, no points; yellow, deducts 1 point; and black is a forfeit color which rules a player out of the game.

The players form a line around and just outside the circle of cups, with a distance of about 2 feet between players. When the leader says "March" they start to march at an even, brisk

pace around the circle. At short intervals the leader, with his
back turned to the players, blows a short blast on a whistle.
At the first sound of the whistle, the marchers must stop
immediately. Any player who stops before the whistle is
blown or moves after it has been blown is out of the game. As
soon as the leader has blown the whistle, he turns around and
awards points to the players who are closest to the various
"lucky" cups. Should two players be the same distance from a
certain colored cup, both of them are given the number of
points which it represents. The players closest to the black
cups are out of the game. After the award and deduction of
points, the march around begins again. The winning score can
be set at 10, and the first player to gain that number of points
is the winner. Circles may be made larger and cups placed
farther apart when desired.

CHOPSTICKS

FOR BOYS AND GIRLS   2 TO 12 PLAYERS   PLAYED OUTDOORS
ELEMENTARY—SR. HIGH   INDIVID.—TEAM   OR INDOORS

Eating peas with a fork isn't easy! Try to picture an Oc-
cidental woman in an Oriental restaurant attempting to eat
them with chopsticks. Watching her efforts caused the game
of Chopsticks to be devised. Few players will play it chop-
chop.

Two or more players can compete in this amusing game.
Each player requires two thin, flat sticks 6 inches long and 1
inch wide. Spatulas of this size, which may be bought in most
drugstores, do very well. Two paper saucers 5 inches in
diameter and four ordinary marbles complete the equipment
required for each player. This tricky game may be greatly
simplified for younger players by using large marbles or small,
hard rubber balls, 1 or 1½ inches in diameter, instead of
marbles.

On a starting line, a saucer with four marbles in it is placed
for each player; and directly opposite and 20 feet distant, a
second saucer is placed. There should be a 4-foot lane be-

tween saucers. A player stands behind each saucer which contains the marbles. He holds a chopstick in each hand and it must be held by one end.

On the word "Go!" each player picks up one marble, using the ends of his chopsticks. He then races to the saucer opposite him and drops the marble into it. Any marble dropped on the way must be picked up with the chopsticks and put into the saucer at the finishing line before the next marble is carried. In order to have each player run a fair race, the chopsticks must be held by the ends, one stick held in each hand, and not halfway down the stick. The first player to have all four marbles in the saucer on the finishing line is the winner.

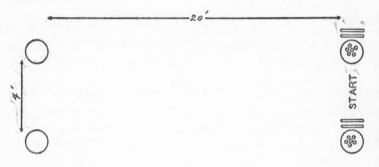

It is fun to play this game as a relay race, two or more players on each team, with an equal number of players at each end of each line of saucers. The second player on each team to carry the marbles does not start back to the starting line saucer with them until all four marbles have been put into the second line saucer by the first player on the team. Each team, of course, uses its own line of two saucers.

This game can be made more difficult by placing the two saucers farther apart or by using additional marbles for each player.

MARBLE TOES

FOR BOYS AND GIRLS   2 TO 12 PLAYERS   PLAYED OUTDOORS
ELEMENTARY—JR. HIGH   INDIVIDUAL   OR INDOORS

Marble Toes was created as a means of introducing tender-feet to the joys of walking on soft, fragrant grass and to cultivate the gift of prehensile toes. It is interesting to note that this was one of the "special request" games keenly contested during a Garden Party Games Program conducted for a woman's social club.

This is an amusing game which some players find easier than Chopsticks. It is played on a lawn, carpet, or clean floor because the players contest in bare feet. The only equipment needed for each player is four ordinary marbles and two paper saucers 5 inches in diameter. The saucers are placed directly opposite each other with a distance of 20 feet between them. There should be a 4-foot lane between saucers at each end of the course. A player stands beside each saucer at the starting end, and four marbles are put into each saucer. Before being used by different players, the marbles should be dropped into an antiseptic solution, in order to prevent any possibility of infection.

On the word "Go!" each player picks up a marble with the toes of the right or left foot and hops on the other foot to the second line of saucers. There he drops the marble into his own saucer and goes back to the starting line for another. Should the marble be dropped on the way, miss the saucer or roll out, it must be picked up with the toes again and put into the saucer before the player returns for another marble. The first player to put all of his marbles into the finishing line saucer is the winner.

This game can be made harder for older groups by putting the saucers farther apart or adding an extra marble or two to each plate.

LITTLE MISS MUFFETT

FOR GIRLS   3 TO 10 PLAYERS   PLAYED OUTDOORS
ELEMENTARY—JR. HIGH   INDIVIDUAL   OR INDOORS

This game was thought up to put an additional streak of action to the "creep up quietly" category of games. Though many boys are quite willing to creep up and surprise Little Miss Muffett, not one of them ever volunteers to play the part of the heroine of the tale, despite their boasts of being dead shots with ball and elastic. Something had to be done about it—and so Boone Ball, which follows this game, was devised for the boys. This is how Little Miss Muffett is played.

One of the girls plays Little Miss Muffett and sits quietly on her "tuffet," which is a paper-plate marker placed on the ground, in the middle of a circle 30 feet in diameter. This circle is outlined on the ground or floor. She is surrounded by the other players, the spiders, who stand just outside the circle. The spiders try to touch Miss Muffett on either shoulder, approaching her one at a time. She is armed to meet all attacks with a trusty "weapon," made by fastening a small sponge rubber, or paper, ball about 1½ inches in diameter to one end of a thin piece of elastic, 4 or 5 feet long when not stretched. Should no elastic be available, balls made from rolled-up paper tied to a 6-foot length of light string will serve. Miss Muffett holds the end of the elastic or string while throwing the ball.

When a leader gives the "Attack!" signal, the spiders attack, one by one. Should one of the spiders manage to get safely past Miss Muffett's weapon and touch her on the shoulder, that player takes Miss Muffett's place. The leader may decide that Miss Muffett can put three spiders, or more, out of business before another player takes her place.

Instead of using one ball attached to the elastic, Miss Muffett can be given six small paper or sponge rubber balls which are not tied to elastic or string. These balls are thrown at the attackers and each one who is hit is out of the game.

When the heroine has thrown all of the balls, they may be returned to her.

BOONE BALL

FOR BOYS	3 TO 10 PLAYERS	PLAYED OUTDOORS
ELEMENTARY	INDIVIDUAL	OR INDOORS

In this game, Daniel Boone is armed with the same sort of weapon as the one used in the preceding game, a sponge rubber ball attached to a 5 or 6 foot length of elastic which stretches easily. Instead, he can be given six small balls made from rolled pieces of paper, which he throws at his attackers. They will not return to him like the sponge rubber ball on the elastic but they can be gathered up and returned to him after his ammunition is expended.

Daniel kneels on a paper-plate marker in the middle of a circle 30 feet in diameter, while the Indians crouch just outside the circle outline, which should be marked on the ground, waiting for the signal to attack.

When the leader says "Attack," the Indians steal up on Daniel, one by one, and try to tag him before they bite the dust as the result of a well-placed shot from his trusty gun. All Indians who are hit retire at once from the game and Daniel Boone may continue to fire until he is tagged by an attacker, whereupon the Indian who made the successful attack takes over the weapon. A smart Indian may tempt Daniel to shoot, then dodge and tag the pioneer before he has the chance to reload. A leader may have the Indians attack two or three at a time, but in this case of a mass attack the intrepid outdoorsman stands little chance.

Another version of the game, for older players, is to have Boone blindfolded, but with ears uncovered, and while so handicapped take on the attackers one at a time, locating and shooting the stealthily attacking braves by keen "earsmanship" coupled with good marksmanship.

A good leader always follows the fashion trend in popular

heroes, and Daniel Boone can become Davy Crockett without affecting the marksmanship too greatly.

OKOTOKS

FOR BOYS   2 TO 10 PLAYERS   PLAYED OUTDOORS
ELEMENTARY—SR. HIGH   INDIVID.—TEAM

This game is adapted from a popular game of the Blackfoot Indian boys and men in which they see who can throw a big round stone between the legs the farthest. They call the sport "Throwing the Okotoks." In this version, a basketball or soccer ball takes the place of the stone.

The player throwing the ball stands with his legs apart and his heels touching a line marked on the ground. He throws the ball as far as he can between his legs, stooping and using both hands. A certain skill is required to make the ball travel in a fairly straight line and go as far as possible before touching the ground, because the length of the throw is decided by where the ball first touches the ground after it leaves the player's hands. Individual players contest as well as teams of two to five boys.

Since a ball is used in this form of the game, the players may also compete in throwing the ball for height, from the same position used when throwing for distance. The ball will not go very high when thrown from this position, and the leader will be able to judge which are the highest throws in order to decide on the winning team or player.

MAIL CARRIER

FOR BOYS AND GIRLS   4 TO 16 PLAYERS   PLAYED OUTDOORS
ELEMENTARY—JR. HIGH   INDIVID.—TEAM

Little equipment is needed for this observation game. Eight or ten large-size matchboxes, about 5 by 2½ inches, with a slit to receive letters cut in each of them, as shown in the diagram, and about fifty pieces of thick paper or cardboard measuring

2 inches by 4 inches, representing letters, will take care of a
large group of players.

This game is best played outdoors and is not recommended
as an indoor game because, when it is ended, the house or
clubhouse may look as though it has survived, with difficulty,
a strenuous Treasure Hunt.

The Post Office may be a big stump or fallen tree trunk
situated in the middle of a 100-foot square of lightly wooded
country. The postmaster gives each mail carrier from four to
six letters with a different name written plainly on each. The
names should be printed in ink, or typewritten, beforehand,
and the initials of each mail carrier should also be marked
on the back of each of his letters, for letter identification
purposes.

Before the game begins and when nobody is around, the
postmaster with the assistance of a leader or counselor, conceals the number of letter boxes which he has decided to use,
remembering that there must be one mailbox for each name
on the letters. Six names mean six mailboxes.

The mailboxes should be painted or colored in a manner
that blends well into the background against which they are
concealed. Different shades of brown, green, and beige, either
solid colors or used in camouflage patterns, are hard to spot
when hidden on low branches of trees, on stumps, in a thin
clump of bushes, or set into a sandbank. The boxes must not
actually be hidden in the real sense of the word, as they
should be visible to keen eyes without any climbing, digging,
or parting of heavy clumps of bushes in order to reveal their
hiding places. The mailboxes should be placed in spots rang-

ing from ground level to not more than 5 feet above the ground, and lower if the mail carriers are little fellows. The boxes should also be concealed with the mail slits conveniently placed so that the mail carriers do not have to take the boxes from their original places in order to push the letters inside. It is also wise to put the boxes, insofar as possible, in places which are sufficiently screened by trees and foliage to allow the mail carriers to find fairly good cover when delivering the mail, so that they do not reveal the hiding place of the mailbox to rival mail carriers.

Before setting out on their rounds, the mail carriers should be warned not to move the mailboxes, as any mail carrier seen doing so by an inspector will be ruled out of the game. The first mail carrier to return to the post office after having delivered all of his letters correctly is the winner. Whether the letters have all been distributed correctly or not is soon decided when the mailboxes are brought in by the leader after the game and the letters in each box checked to see that the name on the letters inside corresponds with the name on the mailbox. Should letters have been placed in the wrong boxes, the initials of the mail carrier on the back of each letter will reveal the mail carrier who is responsible for errors in delivery. A time limit of an hour or less adds to the fun and excitement.

8.

Games Requiring No Equipment

REUNION

FOR BOYS AND GIRLS   5 TO 15 PLAYERS   PLAYED OUTDOORS
ELEMENTARY—JR. HIGH   PARTNER—TEAM

All players pair off, each pair being a partner-team. One player, the guard, stands about 20 feet in front of the first pair of players with his back turned toward them. The other teams of twos line up behind the first pair, in double file. The first pair in line, on a signal from the leader, run forward together, passing as closely as they dare, one on each side of the guard. They try to join hands after they have passed the guard safely, and as close to him as possible. The guard must not move before one runner at least is level with him. He then tries to touch either of the partners before they can join hands ahead of him. Should he succeed in touching one of the runners, that player becomes the guard.

When the two players manage to link up without either one being tagged, they fall in at the end of the line for another try when their turn comes around again.

Only one team runs forward at a time, its turn being decided by its place in the line.

ONE MINUTE TO GO

FOR BOYS AND GIRLS   3 TO 30 PLAYERS   PLAYED OUTDOORS
JR. HIGH—SR. HIGH   INDIVID.—TEAM   OR INDOORS

This is a good game to impress on the players the duration of one minute. The contestants may compete either as individual players or as two teams, each with the same number of

players. The team form of the game often causes more amusement than the individualistic efforts, owing to the diversity of
opinion among team members as to just how quickly a minute
passes.

A start and finish line are marked on the ground opposite
each other and 40 feet apart. The players line up behind the
starting line. When the leader says "Go!" they start to walk
very slowly—if they hope to win—to the finish line. The catch
is that the time spent on the short walk must be as close to one
minute—no more and no less—as a player, or team, can esti-
mate; only the leader may look at his watch or stop watch.
There should be no coaching from the side lines and the face
of any clock on the wall should be screened during the game.

A strict rule of the game, which adds to the fun, is that once
the signal to start is given, each player must begin and keep
on walking, no matter how slowly, until the finish line is
reached. Players who merely stand still are ruled out of the
game. At the rate of progress, it is quite hard for the leader or
umpire to judge whether players are moving or standing still.
To watch some of the participants walking in slow motion
provides amusement for the onlookers.

The individual players, or team leader, may use one of the
various ways of calculating the passage of a minute, such
as repeating certain words or phrases so many times in sixty
seconds, but the formulas must not be repeated aloud.

When this game is played in a small room, the distance
can be increased by having the players turn around when they
reach one end of it and then continue to walk back to the
other end, where the walk finishes. This turnabout does not
make the event any easier.

ROYAL COACH

FOR BOYS AND GIRLS	6 TO 20 PLAYERS	PLAYED OUTDOORS
ELEMENTARY	INDIVIDUAL	OR INDOORS

This game is played in various forms by children in England. The players either sit in a circle or in two or three lines.

All of the players in the line formation face in the same direction. The leader gives each player either the name of a royal personage, some part of the royal regalia, the name of one of the four horses, or the name of some part of the harness. One player is the coachman, one the coach, and so on. For instance: King, Queen, Prince, Princess, Duke, Duchess, Lady Jane, Lady Joan, Lord Irving, Lord Irwin, the crown, scepter, cushion, coachman, coach, horn, the horses—Dare, Darby,

Dark, and Dart—the bridle, reins, traces, and other additions if needed, so that all of the players have a name. It will be seen that the lords and ladies, horses too, have somewhat similar names, so that they have to be on the alert and not carry out an action at the wrong time, especially such an action as will rule them out of the game.

The leader stands in the middle of the circle or in front of the lines of players and calls out the name of a person or object one by one and in any order, more or less. Each player stands up promptly when called and sits down after he has made the correct motion. The King salutes, with his left hand; the Queen bows graciously; the Prince and Princess raise their left hands in greeting; the Duke, Duchess, lords, and ladies also bow graciously, but more deeply than the Queen does; the coachman touches the brim of his imaginary hat; each horse stamps its feet impatiently three times; all of the royal regalia pieces—crown, scepter, etc.—turn completely around to the right; the coach and all parts of the harness turn completely around to the left. When a leader plays this game for the first few times, a list of characters and things and the motions they carry out may be found helpful.

The game can be improved by the leader telling an improvised or prepared story which mentions each person and object several times, and sometimes at unexpected places, in a plausible tale. Mention can be made of the Royal Family, the Ladies, the Lords, the horses and the coach and harness, so that several players have to go through their motions at the same time. All players who fail to do so drop out of the game.

A leader can add amusement to the game and keep the players guessing at the same time by calling out names at unexpected places, naming two or three horses and then a personage, when another horse is ready to jump up, for instance. Should a person, horse, or other object rise out of turn or by mistake, that player is ruled out of the game.

Another way to play Royal Coach is to have all of the players follow the leader in any order and in single file while he slowly leads them around in a big circle. He calls out the name of a personage or object as they march. The person or object mentioned must run immediately to the head of the line and fall in directly behind the leader, calling out, "the King is here," "Lady Jane is here," "the coach is here," and so on, as he takes his place directly behind the leader. When the leader calls for the Royal Family there is a well-mannered rush, quite different from the stampede which takes place when the leader calls for the horses.

The simpler way to play this game for younger players is to have each player simply stand up and turn around twice, in any direction, then sit down, instead of making the varied motions.

LATCH ON!

FOR BOYS AND GIRLS   5 TO 10 PLAYERS   PLAYED OUTDOORS
ELEMENTARY—JR. HIGH   INDIVIDUAL

Four players stand in line one behind the other and hold each other either by the back of the belt or at the waist, but not around it. They start to run in a zigzag manner while a fifth player tries to hitch on to the waist of the last player in the line. The players, by sharp turns and dodging, make it as difficult as possible for him to latch on, but the line must not become broken at any point. When the fifth player hitches on, the same efforts are made to prevent all of the remaining players from latching on. After the last player has managed to connect, each player gets a chance to lead from the head of the line.

WILLY, NILLY, RED, GREEN, BLACK

FOR BOYS AND GIRLS   12 TO 18 PLAYERS   PLAYED INDOORS
ELEMENTARY—JR. HIGH   INDIVID.—TEAM   OR OUTDOORS

A request for a quiet game for classroom use which would keep the players on the alert while it was being played brought Willy, Nilly, Red, Green, Black into being.

This quick-moving game keeps the players on the *qui vive*. There should be the same number of players on each team. The teams each form a crescent facing each other. The player at one end of each crescent is called "Willy" and the player at the other end of each crescent is named "Nilly." Each of the other players is given the name of a color, in any order— red, green, black, white, brown, yellow, orange, purple, aqua, gray, mauve, etc. After the leader has told each player the color he represents, he must make certain that each player knows his color.

Willy starts the game by calling "Willy—Red," or any other color he wishes. Red must instantly call out "Red—Yellow," or any other color which comes first to mind. Each player must call out his own color before naming a second color. Each color named calls his own color and then another color, and the game proceeds. A player who calls the colors wrongly or fails to respond immediately when his color is called is ruled out of the game.

Neither Willy, Nilly, nor any other color can be repeated immediately after it has just been called. As an example, Willy can call "Willy–Nilly," but Nilly cannot reply "Nilly–Willy." He must call the name of a color after calling his own name. Speed is urged by the leader in order that the game be played fairly and well. Calling the colors in the wrong order, as in the case of a player who inadvertently names the color he is calling before mentioning his own color, puts him out of the game. The same thing happens when a player mentions a wrong color instead of his own, replies to a color call which is not his, or calls a color which has been called just before his turn. The leader should see that all of the different colors are called fairly often, not only the colors easiest to think of in a hurry, so that all players have a chance to participate.

After a few minutes of play, when teams compete, the winning team is the one which has the greatest number of players still in action, or the game may go on until only one team remains. When the game is played as an individual contest, the last few players may be considered winners by a tie.

CELEBRITIES

FOR BOYS AND GIRLS	4 TO 20 PLAYERS	PLAYED INDOORS
ELEMENTARY—SR. HIGH	INDIVIDUAL	OR OUTDOORS

This game can provide a good deal of fun in addition to being not too noticeably educational, especially if the "celebrities" interviewed are suitable for the age group which plays the game and the interviews are entirely impromptu ones. Along educational lines, when older groups are playing, the game may take the form of an interview of someone in the news at the moment or a well-known explorer or author, past or present, the player interviewed pretending that he is the person in question. The interviewer must work as hard as the one interviewed in order to keep the interview moving at a fast pace along interesting lines. In order to choose suitable players for the two roles, the leader should have some idea of the interests and knowledge of the participating players.

On the lighter side, especially for younger players, imaginary people or fairy folk can be interviewed. Clowns, movie stars, circus performers, and "inventors" also provide good subjects.

Older groups frequently provide alert and witty reporters who, when played up to by the person being interviewed, can conjure up at a moment's thought situations which are both interesting and hilarious.

SING SONG STOP

FOR BOYS AND GIRLS	2 TO 14 PLAYERS	PLAYED INDOORS
ELEMENTARY—JR. HIGH	INDIVIDUAL	OR OUTDOORS

In this little musical game the leader sings or hums the melody of a well-known song. The players hum along with him as soon as they recognize the tune. The leader stops suddenly and unexpectedly, at any point. The players must stop immediately. Any player who continues to hum after the leader stops is out of the game. The player who follows and stops correctly and is the last remaining player is the winner. If the leader can play the harmonica, he may use it instead of humming, and the piano also makes an excellent stop-and-go musical medium. Players who are familiar with the latest songs should be given a chance to lead this game.

USE YOUR HEAD!

FOR BOYS AND GIRLS　　　　6 TO 20 PLAYERS　　　　PLAYED INDOORS
ELEMENTARY—JR. HIGH　　　　INDIVIDUAL　　　　OR OUTDOORS

This game was originated for this book not so much with the idea of creating a new game as for the purpose of suggesting just how "Find the Leader" should be played in order to secure the maximum of suspense and fun.

It is a new version of the game originally known as "Guess the Leader" or "Spot the Leader." Nearly always, the directions given for playing the similar game omit the most important rule. No mention is made of the fact that the spotter must turn slowly, or quickly if he will, in order to give the player who is leading the movements a sporting chance to make a change while the spotter is not looking in his direction.

To play this game, the player who is to lead the various motions is pointed to by the leader while the spotter in the middle of the circle of players, or just outside it, has his eyes covered. The player pointed to by the leader raises his hand to let the leader know that he understands and will lead the motions. While the spotter still has his eyes covered, the player who leads begins a motion which is immediately copied by the other players, and the leader of the game asks the spotter to get busy and spot the leader of the game. As the title of the game indicates, all of the motions must be made with the head, while the spotter turns around in the middle of the circle and tries to detect who is leading the motion. A considerable number of amusing changes can be made, though only the head is used. The player who leads the changes may nod his head, tilt it backward and forward, to the left or right, front to left, front to right, and so on. Then the head may be turned in as close to a complete half circle as possible or in any other way the leader indicates.

Because of the unintentional yet most amusing way that some of the players always make certain motions, such as shaking the head sadly when the spotter looks at them, a hazard may be added to this game. Any player who smiles may be ruled out of the game, and 5 points may be deducted from the winning score of 10 points from the spotter who smiles before he succeeds in pointing out the leader of the changes.

CROSS STEP BALANCE RACE

FOR BOYS AND GIRLS   4 TO 18 PLAYERS   PLAYED OUTDOORS
ELEMENTARY—JR. HIGH   INDIVID.—TEAM

For this amusing game, two lines are marked on the ground 30 feet apart, on a smooth, grassy area. These lines may be marked with lime, or tape or white paper-plate markers stapled to the ground. The players stand behind the starting line and face the finishing line.

When the leader says "Go!" each player swings his right foot so that it crosses in front of the toes of the left foot, bringing the heel of his right foot against the outer side of the left foot to a point about halfway between the heel and toe. Players must keep their feet pointing straight ahead as they advance. Now, as quickly as possible, the left foot is swung in front of and then alongside the outer side of the right foot, placing the heel against the outer side at a point halfway between the heel and toe. This alternate change of step is continued until the winning line is reached.

This game can also be played by teams of two, with one player standing behind each line. When the first player to start reaches the second line, his partner takes off on the return trip to the starting point. One lane of players races against the others, and the first team to complete the course correctly is the winner.

Cross Step Balance Race may also be run in the way described above, with two or three players starting from each line, as a relay race.

HEEL AND TOE

FOR BOYS AND GIRLS   3 TO 12 PLAYERS   PLAYED OUTDOORS
ELEMENTARY   INDIVID.—TEAM

For this balance race, two lines are marked on the ground 30 feet apart. The players stand behind the starting line, with about 4 feet between players.

On the word "Go!" each player places the heel of the right foot directly in front of the left foot, with the right heel touching the left toe. Then, without losing balance, he brings the left foot around directly in front of the right, with the left heel touching the right toe. He continues as quickly as possible in this way until he reaches the finish line. Should a player lose his balance, have to touch the ground for support, or lift a foot high in air to maintain balance, he must turn and go back 2 paces before continuing the race.

This makes a good race or relay race for two or more teams, each team using a separate lane and the members either starting the race at the same line or dividing so that half of the players start from different lines.

LOW BRIDGES

FOR BOYS OR GIRLS   10 TO 30 PLAYERS   PLAYED OUTDOORS
ELEMENTARY—JR. HIGH   INDIVID.—TEAM

This game should be played on smooth, grassy ground or at least on flat, clean ground which has been inspected before play, so that the area is clear of any sharp objects.

An even number of players stand in a circle, with 4 feet between players, and number from 1, indicated by the leader, to the highest number in the circle. The leader then asks the odd numbers to face inward toward the center of the circle, while the even numbers all face around the circle in the same direction, decided by the leader. A paper-plate marker 6 inches in diameter is placed on the ground just outside the circle between player 1 and the last even-number player. This marker indicates the starting point of the race.

The players on each side of the marker go down on hands and knees facing each other, and wait for the word to start. On the "Go!" signal they crawl as fast as possible beneath each bridge formed by the legs of the other players until they arrive back at the starting marker. There is a catch in this

⊖= MARKER
●O= TEAMS

game, however, which adds considerably to the time required by the players to circle the circle. The hitch lies in the fact that players must crawl *headfirst* through the first bridge they come to and crawl *backward* through the second bridge. The race continues in this way, the players reversing ends at each bridge, until they arrive back at the starting point. The first player to arrive there is the winner.

There is always added fun and excitement at the point in the circle where the two racing players meet more or less head on, especially if they meet under a bridge. The next two players in the circle can start the race from their places in the circle and finish at the place from which they started. The other players can also start from the points which they occupy in the ring. The distance covered by each crawler is the same as that covered by the first two contestants, as each player makes a complete circle under the bridges. It is helpful if the leader changes the position of the marker plate to indicate the order in which each contesting pair races. The race continues completely around the circle until all players have had a chance.

This game makes an amusing relay race with one half of the circle racing against the other half, even if the race is crawled in headfirst fashion throughout. Each even number is touched off by the arrival back in place of the even number who races ahead of him. When that player gets back into his original place—but not before—he shouts "Two through!" or "Four through!" according to his number, which is the signal for the next even number to take off. The odd numbers call "One through!" or "Three through!" as the case may be, as a signal for the next odd number to start. The last man of a team to arrive back in his position first indicates the winning team.

DRESSED FOR THE BALL

FOR GIRLS   4 TO 12 PLAYERS   PLAYED INDOORS
ELEMENTARY—JR. HIGH   INDIVIDUAL   OR OUTDOORS

The players sit in a circle around a leader. They may speak of any articles of clothing and adornment, but two or three colors are chosen, such as green, gold, or aqua, which must not be mentioned. A bouquet, flowers, perfume, gloves, and similar things are accepted. No article of clothing or adornment may be mentioned more than once, and each player must only mention one thing at a time.

The leader may start the game by asking one of the girls in the circle, "How was Susan dressed for the Ball?" The player may reply, "Susan wore a blue silk dress." She must not go into further detail, so the other players may have a chance of using their imagination in describing the trimming and other decoration. The game continues clockwise around the circle. Each player who cannot answer quickly, names a forbidden color, or mentions an article for the second time is ruled out of the game.

9.

Relay Races and Relay Games

IN ALL RELAY RACES leaders should constantly be on the lookout, when one player touches off another, in order to prevent collisions between the returning runner and the one about to take his place. The players waiting to be touched off should stand in a line, one behind the other and slightly to one side or just behind where each runner finishing his section of the race arrives. Such an arrangement permits them to be started off speedily without the risk of being run down. Usually the next runner in line is so eager to be touched off at the soonest possible second that he will run out a few steps to meet the incoming runner. Because of this, the leader should warn runners in advance that the runner who runs out in front of the arriving runner, in order to speed up the touch off, will be disqualified, as such tactics are unfair. Since disqualification of a runner means disqualification of his team, the waiting runners, warned in advance, will not take such chances.

BRIDGE PASS RELAY

FOR BOYS OR GIRLS	10 TO 30 PLAYERS	PLAYED OUTDOORS
ELEMENTARY—JR. HIGH	TEAM	OR INDOORS

The gear required for this amusing game is two tennis balls or balls of similar size and a paper-plate marker 6 inches in diameter.

The players form a circle with an arm's length between players. The leader places the plate marker between any two players in the circle. Each of these players becomes Number

1 player on one team. The players on the left of one Number 1 player and the players on the right of the other Number 1 player count off from 2 upward, according to the number of players on each team. There should be the same number of players on each team, and each half of the circle is a team which faces in the same direction as its Number 1 player. All players in the circle stand in a feet-astride position. The leader gives a ball to each Number 1 player.

On the word "Go!" each Number 1 player steps inside the circle and passes the ball from hand to hand under the bridge formed by the legs of the player directly in front of him. Both players continue in this way, in opposite directions, completely around the circle until they return to their original positions. The ball must not be allowed to touch the ground and if it is dropped, it must be picked up and taken back two bridges as a forfeit. As soon as the Number 1 player has completed the circuit, he hands the ball to the second player, who continues the race over the same course. The relay continues in this fashion until each player on each team has circled the circle. The last player on a team to finish first decides the winning team, and upon his arrival back in his original place he calls out his number to announce the victory of his team.

The most amusing part of this game happens each time two players from rival teams meet at or under a bridge!

BALL WEAVE RELAY

FOR BOYS AND GIRLS	6 TO 30 PLAYERS	PLAYED OUTDOORS
ELEMENTARY—JR. HIGH	INDIVID.—TEAM	OR INDOORS

This is a game devised by the author to develop flexibility of the back muscles and promote quickness of hand. Although it can be played as a competitive game between two teams, there is a lot of fun in it when played as an individual event.

When there are only six or eight players, they may form a crescent, facing forward and standing with their feet about 12 inches astride and each foot about 12 inches distant from that of their neighbors on either side. The leader gives a volleyball or basketball to the player on the left end of the line, as he faces it. On the word "Go!" the player with the ball bends forward, places the ball on the ground directly in front of him, then pats it back behind him, between his legs, with the right hand. He pushes it slightly toward the left so that he can reach it easily with the fingers of the left hand and pat it forward to just in front of his left toe, whereupon his neighbor, on the left, is ready to do exactly the same thing just as soon as the ball is in position. This continues to the end of the line where the last player goes through the same motions but in addition pats the ball back to just in front of his right toe. Here his neighbor takes over but this time he pats the ball back with his left hand and forward with his right hand, and the same movements are made by the other players to the end of the line. With a little practice, this game can be played very quickly, and each player must be on the alert to keep the ball moving without one wasted second or movement Should a player pat the ball out of his reach, he can be ruled out of the game, as the ball must be kept in motion, up and down the line, without players changing the position of their feet.

Competition between two teams is carried out by having two teams of equal size face each other in straight lines about 6 feet apart, with the players on each team standing as described above. The ball can be started at opposite ends of each line, so that the sequence of movement is the same for both teams and the weaving relay is run three times along the line. The team which succeeds in getting the ball back first at the end of the third trip decides the winning team. A team patting the ball out of reach at any point of the line can be disqualified, or lose points, as decided by the leader.

For real exercise, it is suggested that this game be played occasionally with tennis balls, or rubber balls about that size.

OVER AND BACK

FOR BOYS AND GIRLS   8 TO 16 PLAYERS   PLAYED OUTDOORS
ELEMENTARY—JR. HIGH   TEAM   OR INDOORS

This is a variety relay played by two or more teams with
four players on each. The teams stand in line, one player
behind the other. The first player on each team faces a line
drawn on the ground or marked with paper-plate markers, 30
feet away. There should be a lane of about 4 feet between
teams.

Each player must run to the mark opposite and return, to
touch off the next player. The catch is that each of the four
players must move to the mark and back in a different way
from the player or players ahead of him. Each player, of
course, uses the same movement in both directions. Any member of a team who uses the same movements as another member of his team disqualifies his team. This does not apply to
the method of progression used by the members of the other
teams, but each team should try to think up original methods
of locomotion and not copy another team, if possible. Since
each team is racing against the others, the difficulty lies in
each player thinking of the fastest yet most original way of
making the round trip. Players may run forward, backward,
sideways, travel on all fours, provided they can make good
time that way, hop in various ways, or jump in any manner
they like during this race.

KANGAROO RELAY

FOR BOYS AND GIRLS   10 TO 30 PLAYERS   PLAYED OUTDOORS
ELEMENTARY—JR. HIGH   TEAM   OR INDOORS

Two teams of equal size stand in two lines 2 paces apart.
Each line faces in the same direction and there should be an
arm's length between players in line. The first player in each
line holds a stout pole about 3 feet in length. When each team
has been told what to do and is ready, the game leader calls
"Go!"

Immediately, the first player in each line holds out one end of his stick to player Number 2, holding the other end in his right hand while the second player holds his end of the stick in his left hand. Stooping close to the ground these two players run down the line of teammates, holding the stick as close to the ground as possible. Each player in line jumps, with both feet together, over the stick as it reaches him.

When the two stick-bearing players reach the end of the line, player Number 1 takes the place at the end of the line, while player Number 2 runs back to the head of the line, taking the stick with him. He holds out the end of the stick to the first player now in line, and once again the stick is taken down the line while the other players jump over it as before.

This relay continues until once again the Number 1 player stands at the head of the line. The team wins whose Number 1 player is first at the head of his file of players, as at the start of the race, provided each player on that team has jumped the stick cleanly each time it went down the line. Few rules are required for this game but a leader may count points against, or disqualify, a team whose players fail to jump over the stick cleanly too often. Naturally, the clumsiness of team members is a handicap to the team which will probably cause it to lose the race in any case.

HOOP PASS RELAY

FOR BOYS AND GIRLS   8 TO 20 PLAYERS   PLAYED INDOORS
ELEMENTARY—JR. HIGH   TEAM   OR OUTDOORS

The only gear required is a smooth, light wooden hoop about 2 feet in diameter for each team competing.

Teams of from four to ten players form in two straight lines, facing each other, with 3 feet between players. The player chosen to run first in each line is given a hoop. On the word "Go!" the player with the hoop holds it with both hands, lowers it, and passes it up over the legs and body of the next player, who must quickly step into it when it is lowered to ground level. The hoop holder then brings it up over the player until it is clear of his head. He then continues to the next player, who steps into the hoop, and the game continues as before until the last player in line has gone through the hoop. The Number 1 player then runs to the second player in line and gives him the hoop, taking his place at the head of the line as soon as he has turned over the hoop. Number 2 player begins with Number 1 player and the relay continues as before until each player on the team has had a turn to use the hoop. The first team to finish correctly is the winner.

This is one of the games which helps to develop team spirit, as it is surprising how much co-operation is required on the part of each team member, since an elbow inadvertently stuck out at the wrong moment, or a misstep getting into the hoop, can set a team back considerably.

A variation of this game can be played by having the hoop passed from the head to the feet of the players, or by having the hoop passed first from the head to the feet and then from the feet to the head, alternating with each player.

CIRCLE CIRCLE RELAY

FOR BOYS AND GIRLS	12 TO 32 PLAYERS	PLAYED OUTDOORS
ELEMENTARY—SR. HIGH	TEAM	OR INDOORS

This game is the first of a series of three relay races which are best run with the players in two separate circles, the circles being about 4 feet apart, to eliminate the possible danger of two players colliding during the race. Each team has its own circle and the players on each team stand 1 long pace apart facing inward toward the center of their circle. The leader points out the player in each team who runs first. These players should stand opposite each other as shown in the diagram. A paper-plate marker should be stapled to the ground halfway between the two circles to mark the starting point of the race.

On the word "Go!" each first player races as fast he he can, clockwise, around the outside of his circle. Immediately the first player of a team finishes the circle and regains his place,

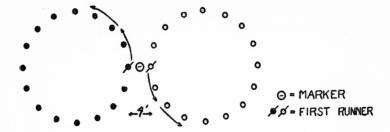

he touches off the second player, who also races around the outside of the circle as the first player did. Each player touches off the player ahead of him until all have circled the circle. The first team to finish wins.

REVERSE CIRCLE RELAY

FOR BOYS AND GIRLS   12 TO 30 PLAYERS   PLAYED OUTDOORS
ELEMENTARY—SR. HIGH   TEAM   OR INDOORS

The players form two circles, as in Circle Circle Relay, but all the players face around the circle in the same direction. The first player to run on each team stands opposite the other, with the marker between them. These players are the Number 1 on each team and they call out their numbers loudly. The other players on the team number from directly behind Number 1, numbering from 2 to the highest number on the team. In this relay, the odd numbers circle the outside of the circle in a clockwise direction, while the even numbers on the team also run outside the circle but in a counterclockwise direction. In this way each player runs in the opposite direction from the runner ahead of him. A player must be on the alert so that when he feels the touch on his shoulder that tells him to run, he runs in the right direction. Players who start out in the wrong direction must return to their original positions in the circle and start their run over again.

A leader can add still another little difficulty to this relay by having the odd numbers go around *outside* the circle in a clockwise direction, while the even numbers run around *in-side* the circle in a counterclockwise direction. The first team to circle its circle correctly is the winner.

CIRCLE PLAYERS RELAY

FOR BOYS AND GIRLS	12 TO 20 PLAYERS	PLAYED OUTDOORS
ELEMENTARY—SR. HIGH	TEAM	OR INDOORS

The players form two circles, as for the preceding relays, and there should be 1 long pace between all players in both circles. The players on both teams face around their circles in the same direction. The player on each team who starts the relay stands at the same point of the circle as shown in the Circle Circle Relay diagram.

On the word "Go!" the Number 1 player on each team runs completely around the player in front of him in a clockwise direction and around the next player in a counterclockwise direction, continuing in this manner around each player until he reaches his own place again. He then touches off the next runner, who races around the circle in the same way. Were it not for these changes of direction, the runners would become so giddy that it is doubtful if they could continue around the entire circle without several stops en route. A game in which the players do not change direction at each player will be found under the not misleading title of Dizzy Circle Relay, in the "Picnic Games" chapter. Naturally, the closer a player can keep to the players when circling them, without actually brushing against them or nudging them out of the circle, the shorter distance he will have to run, but allowing one's self a little leeway in these circlings generally pays off in this relay. The leader should see that all runners do the right thing throughout the race, giving the decision to the first team to circle the circle correctly.

DITCH JUMP RELAY

FOR BOYS AND GIRLS   6 TO 18 PLAYERS   PLAYED OUTDOORS

ELEMENTARY—SR. HIGH   TEAM

For this game, only a volleyball or basketball is required for each team and lengths of tape, or other markers, to indicate the starting line and "ditch."

A starting line is marked on the ground; and 30 feet in front and parallel with it, another line is clearly marked. Four feet beyond this line, a third line is plainly marked. The 4-foot space between these two lines represents the ditch.

Teams of from three to six players form up in single file behind the starting line, with a 4-foot lane between teams. The leader gives the first player in each line a volleyball or basketball.

On the word "Go!" the first player on each team runs to the ditch, jumps over it, and then turns and throws the ball to the second player on his team, who has advanced to the starting line. He, in turn, catches the ball, hurdles the ditch, and then tosses the ball to the next player on his team, who has advanced to the starting line, and the relay continues until the last player has jumped the ditch. The first team lined up behind the ditch is the winner.

This game should be based on the average ability of the players, making the ditch wider or narrower and increasing the distance between the starting line and the ditch, to meet the capabilities of the participants.

HOP TOAD RELAY

FOR BOYS AND GIRLS   2 TO 16 PLAYERS   PLAYED OUTDOORS

ELEMENTARY—JR. HIGH   INDIVID.—TEAM

This not-too-easy and amusing race makes a good team and relay event. The only gear required for each player is a tennis or similar soft rubber ball or a paper one made from three tightly rolled sheets of a standard-size newspaper, tied in shape with a piece of strong twine.

Two lines are marked on the ground 40 feet apart and directly opposite each other. For an individual race, all of the players line up immediately behind one of these lines, facing the other. The leader gives each player a ball and on the warning "Get ready!" they place the ball between the ankles. On the word "Go!" each contestant stoops down, clasps his hands around and just below the knees, and hops in that position, with both feet together, to the line directly opposite. Just as soon as he reaches it, he turns, takes the ball from between the ankles and places it between and just below the knees and, with the hands clasped behind the head, hops back to the starting point. When a player drops a ball or loses balance so that he is forced to touch the ground with a hand, he must replace the ball, hop backward 2 hops, and then continue the race. A player who holds the ball in place at any point during the race is disqualified. The first player to return to the starting point decides the winner.

When there are two or more players on each relay team, an equal number of players lines up behind each of the two lines mentioned above. The first member of each team hops to the second line, with the ball between his ankles. Immediately he is touched off, the second player hops with the ball between his knees, as in the individual contests, and the relay continues until each player has hopped. The few rules set down for the individual race also apply to the relay event. The last player on a team to come in ahead of the last players of other teams decides the winning team.

HANDS UP HOOP RELAY

FOR BOYS AND GIRLS   12 TO 20 PLAYERS   PLAYED OUTDOORS
ELEMENTARY—JR. HIGH   INDIVID.—TEAM   OR INDOORS

The only equipment needed is two light, smooth, wooden hoops as close to 20 inches in diameter as possible and one paper-plate marker. In this, as in all similar hoop games, all rough places on the hoops should be carefully removed by sandpaper or the entire hoop should be wound around with insulating tape to assure an all-round smooth surface.

Two teams of equal size are formed with six to ten players in each. Each team forms a circle and its players all face inward, with an arm's length between players. The paper-plate marker is stapled to the ground halfway between the two circles, as shown in the diagram for Circle Circle Relay. This plate marks the starting point in the race, and the first player on each team. Each first player is given a hoop and when the leader says "Go!" each hoop holder runs into the circle, passes the hoop down over the upraised arms, head, and body of any player except the ones on either side of him, as they must be the last to pass, in any order, through the hoop. When the player with the hoop runs to a player, that player must stretch his hands high above his head, with both arms straight; when the hoop reaches his feet, he steps out of it as quickly as possible and the hoop holder continues on to another player, until everyone in his circle except himself has gone through the hoop. By then, he will have returned to his original place. He now passes the hoop to a player on either side of him who immediately starts into the circle, passing each player through the hoop in his turn. The first team to have each of its players pass the hoop over his teammates is the winner. A variation is to have the hoop holders work from outside the circle.

Played as an individual contest, the player who, with the co-operation of his teammates, finishes ahead of the hoop holder in the rival team, is the individual winner. Players from each team have a turn at being hoop holder, until every member has had a chance.

10.

New Games to Make and Play

THE SIMPLE EQUIPMENT required for the games in this chapter will be found quite easy to make, and the games made will prove durable and well worth the small amount of work needed to add them to the play kit. The few introductory notes which follow will prove helpful, especially as they are applicable to the majority of games covered in this chapter.

CARDBOARD. It should be noted before starting to make most of the games for which cardboard is required that the suggested size for the sheet of cardboard to be used is given as 14 inches by 8½ inches. This is not because it is the best size but because it is a convenient size which is easily procured. A number of games are best made from larger sheets of heavier cardboard, but the 14" x 8½" size is used by laundries when sending back men's shirts and other articles which have been washed. This makes it easy for some arts and crafts counselors to get a supply of such cardboards without expenditure for the material. Two of these cardboards, which are about ⅟₁₆ of an inch thick, glued or pasted together make strong, suitable cardboard sheets for the construction of a number of the games described in this chapter. These reinforced sheets are sturdy and can be worked easily when it comes to cutting and making holes. They can also be painted with show-card paint and other colors without difficulty. Despite these good points, the author uses considerably larger sheets of ⅛-inch thick, white cardboard for his games and demonstrations both at teachers colleges and with children's groups. Actually, almost any size sheet of good quality cardboard from 14″ by 8½″ up to about half as large again will prove satisfactory for the cutout games, provided the proportion of the drawings used is fairly correct.

In cutting heavy cardboard with shears, the work is made easier if a hole about 1 inch in diameter is first cut in the cardboard with a knife or special cutting tool, as a starting point. When improvisation is necessary, a hole may be punched out with an awl or ice pick.

PAINTING. Cardboard can be painted easily and satisfactorily with show-card colors. This paint should be fresh enough to mix easily. When it becomes older and more granular it will color neither lastingly nor well and it is apt to rub off when touched. Ordinary paint or enamel can be used when a brighter and more permanent finish is desired.

Various sets of a game should be painted in different colors for identification purposes. Younger players and older ones too prefer bright colors to drab ones.

The spatulas mentioned in some of the games can be bought at most drugstores—they are used as tongue depressors. A coat of bright paint will add to their appearance and, painted in pairs, most players can have a pair of a different color.

GLUING AND PASTING. After much experimentation, the writer has come to the proven conclusion that strips of strong cotton cloth or tough, heavy paper glued onto the cardboard to form hinges or struts assure a much better and more lasting job than any other kind of adhesive strips. When two pieces of cardboard have to be hinged at the top or sides, they should be held together by these cloth or paper hinges of the right size, glued in position and allowed to dry before painting both cardboard and hinges in the same bright color. Hinges made from tape which has a glossy surface cannot be painted on the outside, and if hinges made from such tape are stuck onto cardboard which has already been painted with show-card paint, they will soon drop off, taking the paint with them. Some medical, cloth adhesive tapes can be fastened to unpainted cardboard to serve as hinges and then the set may be painted. They will wear well enough, although such hinges are generally not as satisfactory as the homemade ones, mentioned above.

DOWELS. All of the dowels mentioned in the games can be made from the standard, round dowels, ranging from ⅛ to ¼ inch, which can be bought quite cheaply in many hardware stores and cut into the lengths required. The dowels should be made of softwood and once they have been cut to size, sandpapered, and rounded at the ends, they can be painted in bright colors. To put the round beads required for some games onto the end of a length of dowel, one end is tapered and forced into an opening in the bead, after a drop of glue has been applied to the tapered end of the dowel. The plain, round, wooden ¾-inch-in-diameter bead is then painted a gay color.

STIFFENING STRING ENDS. In order to stiffen the ends of string so that it can be passed through small holes in cardboard easily and quickly, it is best to dip about ½ inch of the end of the string into paste or liquid glue, then press and shape the end of the string between the thumb and forefinger. This will keep the ends of string from fraying and save a great deal of time when games are being readied just before a play period begins.

CLOWN FACE

| FOR BOYS AND GIRLS | 2 TO 12 PLAYERS | PLAYED INDOORS |
| ELEMENTARY—JR. HIGH | INDIVID.—TEAM | OR OUTDOORS |

A visit to a circus with a group of youngsters sparked the idea for this game. The red rubber ball fastened to the nose of a clown became the center of attraction and formed the focal point of Clown Face.

The clown's face is drawn on a sheet of cardboard 14 inches by 10 inches and ⅛ inch thick. A ½-inch hole is made in the drawing for the clown's nose and a hole ¼ inch in diameter is made in the center of each eye. The teeth and eyebrows are cut out as traps for the small red rubber ball nose and blue marbles, for eyes, which are used in this game. One red rubber ball about 1¼ inches in diameter and two jumbo-size blue marbles are needed. A "pusher" made from a 9-inch length of dowel stick ⅜ inch in diameter, with a ¾-inch round wood bead glued on one end, in the way described under "Dowels" at the beginning of this chapter, and two spatulas 6 inches long also form part of the gear. A paper saucer 5 inches in diameter to hold the ball and marbles completes the equipment.

At least two sets of this game should be made so that individual players or two teams can contest at the same time.

These two sets of Clown Face are placed on the floor about 4 feet apart. Directly in front of each face and 30 feet away a saucer is placed. In this saucer the red ball and two marbles are placed. They are either pushed with the pusher or carried between the points of the two spatulas from the saucer to the face. Playing the game with the spatulas, used as lifters, will be described first.

A player stands beside each saucer holding a lifter, by the end, in each hand. On the word "Go!" he picks up either a marble or the ball and carries it between the *points* of the lifters to the clown's face. When a ball or marble has been placed in its correct position in the face, the player runs back for another, until the face is completed. Any marble or ball dropped between the saucer and the face must be picked up with the lifters and placed in its correct position. Should a marble or ball roll out of place or be pushed out of place, it must be replaced in order to score. The first player to complete the face correctly is the winner.

The drawing shows an additional hazard in the form of a pompom on the clown's hat, which may be added to increase the difficulty of the game if desired. A ½-inch hole is cut in the middle of the pompom into which a second red ball is either carried or pushed.

When two teams of two to six players compete, players on each team take turns, as in a relay race. All of the players except the first must run to the face, collect the marbles, and put them in the saucer at the starting point before starting to race. This may be avoided by having a few spare clown faces on hand and placing one at each end of the game, with the necks toward each other, and the saucer removed. There is less delay in this form of the game, as members of the same team stand behind each clown's face and immediately the face is completed at one end, but not before, a player at that end starts to carry the ball and marbles back to the face at the other end. This continues until all players have completed the face. The first team to do so is the winner.

In playing with a pusher instead of the lifters, the ball and marbles are pushed, one by one, from the saucer to the face. They are pushed with the *bead* on the end of the pusher, not the stick, and the stick must be held upright in one hand. In this version of the game especially, the mouth and eyebrow traps present a considerable handicap. This method is a much easier form of play for younger players, since lifting the marbles correctly between the two lifters and carrying them in that position is a difficult job for even grownups, as adults demonstrate when playing Clown Face.

The author believes in having all play equipment as attractive as possible regardless of the age groups using it. He therefore adds a finishing, though not necessary, touch to each clown's face by pasting patches of strong, colored paper on the back of the cardboard face: white, across the cutout teeth; green, across the cutout eyebrows; red, across the hole cut in the nose; and blue, across the eyes. Instead of colored paper, strong, white paper can be used and then painted from the front side of the face.

CUP AND BALL

FOR BOYS AND GIRLS	2 TO 6 PLAYERS	PLAYED INDOORS
ELEMENTARY—JR. HIGH	INDIVID.—TEAM	OR OUTDOORS

This little game, which amused knights and ladies at the courts of early kings, is as much a matter of skill and good judgment today as it was then. Here is how it is made. Take three cone-shaped, paper drinking cups which measure about 2½ to 3 inches across the top and paste these cups, one inside the other, to reinforce them. Pierce a little hole about ½ inch below the rim of the cup. Thread one end of a strong piece of thin twine 30 inches long through the hole and knot it tightly to the rim. Leave the twine hanging down outside the cup and tie a knot at the very end of the twine. Now take a small, sponge rubber ball about 1½ inches in diameter and tie a piece of thin, strong twine tightly around the ball at its center, leaving enough twine free at each end of the knot to make a small loop about ½ inch in diameter. Through this loop, pass the knotted free end of twine which is hanging down from the cup and tie it. The cup and ball are now joined by the length of twine, as shown in the diagram. The cups may be painted in gay colors to make the game appear more attractive.

This is how the cup and ball are used. The player holds the cup just below the rim, fingers and thumb around the outside of the cup with the index finger resting on the very edge of the rim, outside, to steady the cup. The ball hangs down at the end of the twine. The player now jerks the cup sharply forward and upward into the air so that the ball rises above it and he then tries to catch the ball in the cup as it falls. He will soon be able to catch the ball in the cup fairly often, no matter from what direction or angle it comes. The secret of playing Cup and Ball well is for the player to keep his eye on the ball—not on the cup. Once the players have the idea, they can contest one against the other or form teams of two

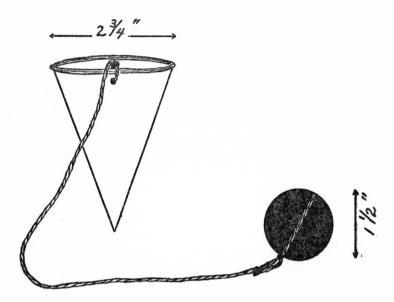

or three players and try a team contest. As this plaything is very easily made, a number of them should be made so that several players can compete at the same time.

An amusing Cup and Ball Race is contested this way:

Players line up behind a line marked on the ground and face another line 30 feet distant. On the word "Go!" the players race for the line opposite but the catch is that each player must put the ball into the cup by tossing it up into the air, using only one hand, three times before the finish line is reached. Whether the player does this right at the start, attempts to do it while running toward the finish line, or just before arriving at the finish line has to be decided by each player, but no player can win without cupping the ball three times between the start and finish lines of the race. This race can be carried out between individual players or between relay teams, with two or more players stationed behind each of the two lines.

MARBLE ARCH

FOR BOYS AND GIRLS   3 TO 10 PLAYERS   PLAYED INDOORS
ELEMENTARY—JR. HIGH   INDIVIDUAL   OR OUTDOORS

The name "Marble Arch" was coined by the author as he watched an intent group of youngsters in London play a nameless game close to the Marble Arch. He noted that the boy who owned the cutout board at which the marbles were rolled, kept all of the marbles which did not roll through the little arches. He did award two marbles to each player who succeeded in rolling a marble through any one of the arches— in spite of which his pockets bulged with the marbles he had won.

The board used for this game should be about 12 inches long and 3 inches wide, and the arches should not be more than 1 inch in width. This arch leaves fair leeway for the passage of a marble, as the average marble measures about ⅝ inch in diameter. The pillar between each arch is 1 inch thick, as shown in the diagram. The game can be made more diffi-

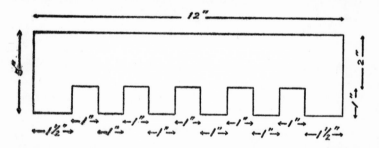

cult by narrowing the arches a little and making the pillars between the arches wider. The board must be held upright and directly facing the line marked on the ground from behind which the marbles are rolled. When the line is marked at short range, 10 or 12 feet away, marbles enthusiasts like to shoot the marbles toward the arches with their thumbs, in the position used when playing the game of marbles. Either this method or rolling the marbles with the hand may be used in Marble Arch. The rolling or shooting distance can be lengthened to meet the skill shown by the average player. Five points can be awarded for each marble which rolls through the arch, and the winning score may be set at anywhere from 20 to 30 points. Players may shoot a single marble or three marbles in succession, as decided by the leader.

To allow more players to compete at the same time without marbles colliding under the arches, a cardboard or wooden box 12 or more inches long and about 6 inches wide may be used instead of the arch board. When the box used is cardboard, the lid is taken off and pasted onto the foot of the box to reinforce it. Arches are then cut in the edges of both sides of the box. A strip of cardboard about 3 inches wide can be glued vertically, lengthwise across the box, dividing it into two equal parts and forming a partition which runs between the arches on the sides of the box. The marbles are thus trapped in the box as they enter from either or both sides and in this way they cannot collide at the arches.

ARCH BALL

FOR BOYS AND GIRLS	3 TO 10 PLAYERS	PLAYED INDOORS
ELEMENTARY—JR. HIGH	INDIVIDUAL	OR OUTDOORS

This game is based on the one called Marble Arch, which precedes it. While it is easier to play, it too requires a steady hand and a sure eye in order to assure a high score. The element of chance in both of these games also counts and helps to make the scoring uncertain and the results amusing. The only equipment needed to play Arch Ball is homemade. A sheet of strong cardboard 18 inches long and 6 inches wide will make the arch, or a more permanent arch can be made by using a sheet of thin wood or plywood instead of cardboard. The arches are cut out as shown in the diagram and squared off, since it is easier to make them that way. The holes shown are large enough for the passage of tennis balls or any balls of about that size, but younger players will have a more

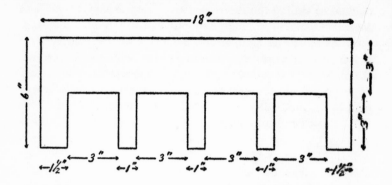

sporting chance if smaller balls, about 1½ inch in diameter, are used.

The rules are simple. Players are allowed either one roll each or three rolls in succession, from a line marked on the floor or ground 20 to 30 feet away. The arch must face the players squarely. The winning score, counting 5 points for each ball rolled through the arches, may be set at 20 or 30 points. This game is equally good fun when played by competing teams.

KNIGHT'S VISOR

FOR BOYS AND GIRLS   2 TO 10 PLAYERS   PLAYED INDOORS
ELEMENTARY—JR. HIGH   INDIVID.—TEAM   OR OUTDOORS

This is a game which the author devised for one of the annual Medieval Days held at The Cloisters, in New York, for children. It is based on a beanbag game but the additional feature which pleased the Knights and Ladies at the Games Tournament is the fact that the closed visor opens on direct hits, allowing the thrown ball to go through and score.

The helmet is cut from a piece of stout cardboard ⅛ inch thick, as shown in the diagram. The hole for the visor is cut out and a piece of cardboard of the same weight is suspended from behind, covering the visor space, leaving 2 inches over at top and bottom and 1 inch at each side. With the cardboard visor cover in this position, a circle of stout paper 1 inch in diameter is pasted or glued over one end of a 3-inch length of stout twine and securely fastened to each side of the helmet, as shown in the drawing. Another circle holds the lower end of the twine to the visor cover, as illustrated. The helmet and front side of the visor cover can be painted realistically in gray, steel blue, silver, or black to represent real armor.

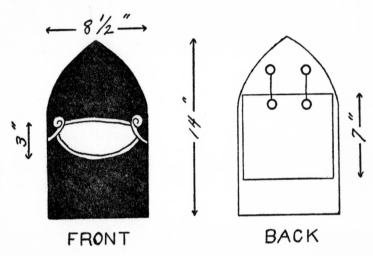

FRONT   BACK

A leader or player holds the helmet upright and steady on a table with the front of the helmet facing the throwing line, marked on the floor, about 15 feet distant. The players try to toss small beanbags or rubber balls, underhand, through the visor opening. The beanbags or balls should not measure more than 2 inches in diameter, and each player may throw either one ball or three balls in succession. Each hit scores 5 points.

TAN-TALIZERS

FOR BOYS AND GIRLS	1 TO 10 PLAYERS	PLAYED INDOORS
JR. HIGH—SR. HIGH	INDIVID.—TEAM	OR OUTDOORS

Long ago, in far-off old China, a wise man named Tan cut seven little pieces of heavy paper out of an exact square of paper and arranged them in many interesting, varied, and amusing figures. Tan had no idea that children and grownups all over the world would still be playing with these puzzling little angles in the Year of the Dragon, four thousand and ninety years later.

The little angles provoke thought and provide fun. Napoleon found this out when he was an island prisoner, and other great men and women have found them equally intriguing. A great number of entirely different figures can be made from the seven angles, as shown in the drawings. By combining two sets, hundreds of designs and figures can be made.

It is fun for each player to make a set and compete in trying to make the best looking house, person, animal, bird, or one of many other things, in the shortest time possible. Two players can work as partners, or two teams of three or more players may contest, using two or three sets of Tan-Talizers, as decided before playing.

The name Tan-Talizers has been coined by the author for this game in order to give full credit to Tan for his ingenious invention, and also to warn players how tantalizing it is to fit the pieces together in the best possible way, in order to give the figures made a lifelike appearance and to create the movement and simple beauty which these little pieces of cardboard can so well portray when they are cleverly arranged at the correct angles.

Players who use their imagination can make dozens of designs, taking care that the pieces fit closely together at all points decided on but *never overlap*. Piece Number 6 in the diagram may be reversed when required but it is the only piece in the set which sometimes needs to be.

In the drawings, the "Mandarin with a Fan" and the "Cat" are made with one set of Tan-Talizers, while the "Man on Horseback" is made by combining pieces from two sets.

The diagram shows a 4-inch square because it provides pieces of a convenient size for play, being neither too large nor too small. However, the sets can be made either larger or smaller, measuring from 2 to 8 inches or more. The one

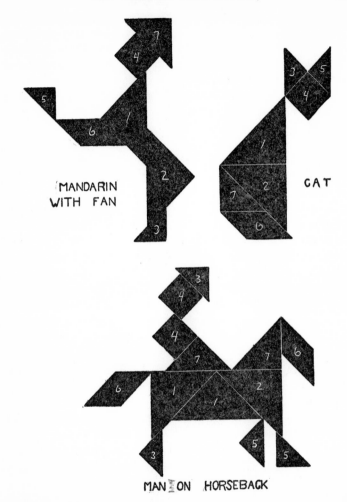

MANDARIN WITH FAN

CAT

MAN ON HORSEBACK

important thing to remember in making Tan-Talizer squares of any size is that the *original* square from which the seven pieces are cut must be an *exact* square, and that the inside line which forms the Number 7 angle is drawn from the exact center of the bottom line to the exact center of the line at the right, shown by the two little dots in the diagram.

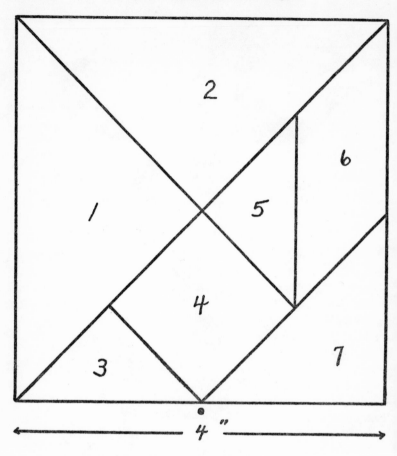

A set of Tan-Talizers is best made from good-quality cardboard. Both sides of the cardboard should be colored black,
with India ink or some other black permanent ink which will
not stain the fingers when the puzzles are used. Cut several
4-inch squares from the cardboard, being very careful to cut
exact squares. The diagram given here is an exact 4-inch
square. It was made so in order that anyone who wishes to
save time may simply trace over it with thin paper, using a
ruler, then place the thin paper over the cardboard and with

ruler and hard pencil rule the lines onto the cardboard. By pressing hard with the pencil, the lines should be marked clearly enough on the cardboard to see easily, and they then can be cut along with a pair of scissors. Once cut out, the angles are ready for use.

SPACE PORT

FOR BOYS AND GIRLS	2 TO 14 PLAYERS	PLAYED INDOORS
ELEMENTARY—JR. HIGH	INDIVID.—TEAM	OR OUTDOORS

Space Port was created to cater to modern youngsters who are interested in Space Men and at the same time to develop the patience required to achieve mundane things before blasting off into outer space.

This modern game is easy to make and good fun to play. The space ship and flying saucer may be colored in bright, fanciful colors, which will not interfere with their flying ability. Show-card colors will serve nicely. The propulsor should be made from heavy cardboard. Although it should not strike the floor when used as a fan to propel the identified flying objects, it often does, so it is well to reinforce the handle end by stapling a spatula on each side, then coloring them. The diagram shows how to make the equipment and also how to set up the game ready for play. Each player requires a propulsor, a space ship, and a flying saucer in addition to a take-off field and a space port. The field and the port should be 30 feet apart and there should be a distance of 4 or 5 feet between the lines of players.

On the words "Blast off!" each player fans one of his flying objects from the field onto the space port. No flying object is considered to have made a landing unless every part of it is directly on the space port. When one object has been fanned into place, the player runs back for the second one, which he also fans onto the space port, after first displacing the object occupying the port with a few waves of the propulsor. The first player to get both flying objects, one at a time, onto the space port is the winner.

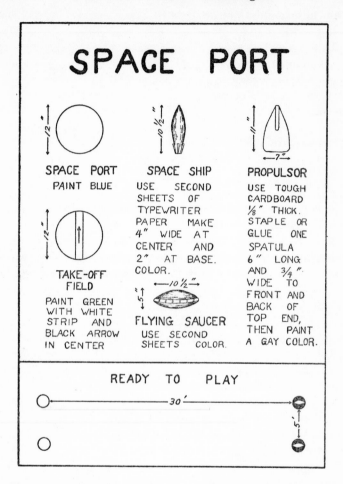

SPACE PORT

SPACE PORT
PAINT BLUE

SPACE SHIP
USE SECOND
SHEETS OF
TYPEWRITER
PAPER MAKE
4" WIDE AT
CENTER AND
2" AT BASE.
COLOR.

PROPULSOR
USE TOUGH
CARDBOARD
⅛" THICK.
STAPLE OR
GLUE ONE
SPATULA
6" LONG
AND ¾".
WIDE TO
FRONT AND
BACK OF
TOP END,
THEN PAINT
A GAY COLOR.

TAKE-OFF
FIELD
PAINT GREEN
WITH WHITE
STRIP AND
BLACK ARROW
IN CENTER

FLYING SAUCER
USE SECOND
SHEETS COLOR.

READY TO PLAY

30'

5'

When playing this game as a team race, with only two players on each team, a player stands behind the take-off field while the other takes up his position behind the space port. In this way no time is lost at either end and when the player has driven both objects from the take-off field onto the space port, the player at the space port end fans them both back, always one at a time, onto the take-off field. The first team to land both objects correctly back at the take-off field is the winner.

This game can also be contested in relay style, with an equal number of players at both the take-off field and space port ends. One player, having completed the one-way flight of both objects, touches off the next player, who continues the race.

NUMBER TOSS

FOR BOYS AND GIRLS	2 TO 16 PLAYERS	PLAYED OUTDOORS
JR. HIGH—SR. HIGH	INDIVID.—TEAM	OR INDOORS

This is a lively sort of improvised tennis game. Two home-made rackets and four cardboard discs are needed for each two players. The rackets are made from two paper plates 9 inches in diameter, glued one inside the other, to reinforce them. Eight discs are cut from cardboard $\frac{1}{16}$ inch thick. The discs are 3 inches in diameter and are glued together in pairs. Painted with yellow or orange show-card paint, they will look well and be highly visible. These four discs are numbered 5, 10, 15, and 0, on one side and in small figures.

Two paper-plate markers are placed on the ground 18 feet apart, or lines may be marked on the ground instead. A player stands behind each marker or line, facing his opponent. Either player has all four discs and he serves for the first round of the game.

The server places one of the discs on his plate and glides it flatly forward with a sharp jerk of the plate. He tries to send the disc fairly high and directly over his opponent's marker. The other player tries to catch the flying disc on his plate, as flatly as possible, so that it will not roll off. He scores the number of points marked on each disc he manages to catch. The real *catch* comes in at this point, as the 0 disc counts 10 points *off* the total score, which is 20, provided the catcher is able to catch all four discs. Since the scoring points marked on each disc are too small to be seen as the discs glide through the air, the players simply try to catch all of them, not having time to worry about which may be the o disc. A player can easily miss a disc or two, or one may roll off his plate after being caught, no matter how hard he tries to catch all of them. Should the o disc be among those missed, that is where the luck comes in.

Players take turns at being the server, and the highest score at the end of four games should decide the winner. Players may run backward to catch discs which glide beyond or to one side of the marker. When players acquire skill in launching the discs, the markers may be placed farther apart, but the distance must suit the serving range of both players.

Number Toss may be played as a team game with two to eight players on each team. In this form of the game each team plays from behind a line marked on the ground at a distance suitable to the serving skill of the players on each team.

ROBOT RACE

FOR BOYS AND GIRLS   3 TO 12 PLAYERS   PLAYED OUTDOORS
JR. HIGH—SR. HIGH   INDIVID.—TEAM   OR INDOORS

In this amusing and exciting race, the winner is decided entirely by chance. The luck of the player who controls the advance of his robot racer decides the issue. The simple equipment required for each player or team is two rather large, heavy-paper drinking cups, not cone-shaped, about 3½ inches high, and four marbles of different colors—red, yellow, white, and black, or any other easily distinguishable colors. In addition, one large paper plate 9 inches in diameter and eight paper disc markers about 4 inches in diameter, or eight cone-shaped drinking cups to take the place of the disc markers, are needed. These markers can be dispensed with if lines are marked on the ground, or floor, to take their place. These lines prove the simplest form of markers when there are a number of players, as the lines can be made long enough to accommodate four or more lines of players.

A shaker, from which the marbles are rolled, is made in

this way: take the two drinking cups mentioned under equipment and put one inside the other. Cut a hole, just a trifle larger than a marble, directly in the center of the bottom of each cup. Now remove the top cup and cover the top of it with a circular piece of opaque cloth, allowing the cloth to hang down outside the cup about 1½ inches. Snap a rubber band over the cloth to hold it in place close to the rim of the cup. Place some liquid glue or paste inside and around the top of the other cup and force the cloth-covered cup down inside it as far as possible, so that the cloth on the top cup is securely held between the cups and the holes in the bottom of both cups are in line and close together. The shaker is now complete. The marbles are fed into the shaker through the hole. The game is now ready to set up and play.

The large paper plates are laid on the ground in a straight line, 3 feet apart. Four of the discs are placed in a straight line, one in front of the other, 18 inches apart, the first marker being placed 18 inches in front of the plate, as shown in the diagram. The remaining four discs are placed directly behind the plate, with 18 inches between the markers and the first marker and the plate, as shown. If the leader wishes, two more disc markers may be added to each end of each line, to lengthen the game.

A player or team of two or three players stands alongside a paper plate; all players face in the same direction toward either set of disc markers. When the players are in position, a leader kneels beside each plate and loads the four marbles into his shaker. A game leader, chosen to direct this game, calls out "Go!" and each leader shakes his cup, then turns it upside down so that only 1 marble rolls out onto the plate. The fall of the marble may require to be controlled by a finger, so that only one marble rolls out at a time. The marble which comes out decides the move to be made. Should the marble be red, the player or team advances two markers. When the marble is yellow, the player goes forward one marker. If the marble is white, the player does not move; and when the black marble comes out, the player goes back two markers. The game leader calls out "Ready, go!" before each move, which warns the leaders to shake and pour one marble. This assures that all players or teams move together and that nobody, in the excitement of the game, gets the advantage of an extra move.

The scoring for Robot Race is easy, as the first player or team to arrive alongside the last marker or line in front of the starting plate is the winner.

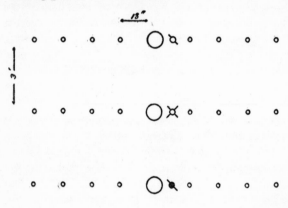

With two or three players on a team, the game is played in relay fashion. When the first player arrives at the last forward marker or line, the next player on the team stands alongside the plate ready to go forward, or back, according to the luck of the shaker. The first team to finish with the most players on the finish line is the winner.

An interesting variation of the game, in which speed on the part of the leaders who handle the shakers may prove an aid, if luck is with them, is to let each leader shake out the moves as fast as he can, without waiting for the words "Ready, go!" from the game leader. The game leader has to be on the alert in this form of the game to see that each leader loads his shaker with *all four* marbles before rolling one out!

The fun and excitement in this game centers around the absolute impossibility for anyone to foresee the moves of players or teams. Sometimes one team will have all of its players backed onto the last marker, and off it, out of the game, while another team will have all of its members lined up at the winning marker in double-quick time.

Though it may take some time to discover the winners when a game is played to a finish, the standing of rival players or teams can always be seen at a glance at any point of the game and, when necessary, games can be decided by that score at any point during play.

DOG HOUSE

FOR BOYS AND GIRLS	2 TO 18 PLAYERS	PLAYED OUTDOORS
ELEMENTARY—JR. HIGH	INDIVID.—TEAM	OR INDOORS

Thought-born in Ireland as the author watched some children try to drive a pig to market, the first version of this game was called "Pigs to Market."* It was devised, through various stages, as the direct result of the children-versus-pig scramble. Now, Dog House, an entirely different game though developed along similar lines, has come into being because of the scene in Donegal.

The time spent in making the simple equipment required for this game will be well repaid in fun. The diagram illustrates the gear needed, and the best materials to use in constructing it are described at the beginning of this chapter. Both kennel and wall have 3-inch-wide upright struts hinged to each end. The fences also are hinged together, as shown in the diagram, with 2-inch squares of cloth or tough paper. These hinges permit the kennel, wall, and fences to spread apart when they are stood on the ground, so they will remain steady. Pointers on painting equipment for games open this chapter.

The "Ready to Play" portion of the drawing shows how the equipment is set up. Before Dog House is played, the leader

* Macfarlan, *New Games for 'Tween-Agers* (New York: Association Press, 1952), p. 33.

should drop each big balloon through the hole in the fence
and the big entrance to the kennel. The small balloons should
be dropped through the small entrance of the kennel, to make
sure that the "pups" are all approximately the same size and
will pass fairly easily through the small hole. It is unfair to a
player if he is given a dog or pup too large to be driven into
the kennel with ease. The game is played as follows.

With two or three players contesting, a player stands beside
each basketful of canines. He must hold the driver vertically,
so that only the bead end is used to drive the dog and pups,
one by one, from the basket, over the fences, through the wall,
and into the kennel. If the dog or any pup misses a fence or
wall and goes around it, it must be driven back in front of the
fence or wall it missed and made to jump the fence or go
through the hole. Just as soon as the dog or pup is in the
kennel, the player runs to the basket for another. The pups
must be driven into the kennel only through the small hole.
Should a pup go into the kennel through the large hole, it
must be poked out and driven into the kennel again through
the small hole. The first player to kennel the dog and pups
correctly is the winner. It does not matter if the dog or pups
roll out of the kennel after being driven inside correctly,
since driving a pup into the kennel can knock others out, or a
slight breeze might blow them out.

A more amusing, exciting, and exasperating version of this
game, when two players are contesting, is to let them use
the same set of fences, wall, and kennel. Each uses his own
starting basket which is in direct line with and 1 foot away
from his opponent's. Each player also uses his own dog and
pups, of course. In this version, especially, the dog and pups
should be of a different color for each player, for identification
purposes. The fun and exasperation come in chiefly when two
canines arrive at a fence, wall, or the entrance to the kennel
at the same moment. A rule for this version of play is that
neither player may strike his rival's dog or pups without pay-
ing the penalty of driving his own canine back one obstacle,
surmounting it, and continuing from there.

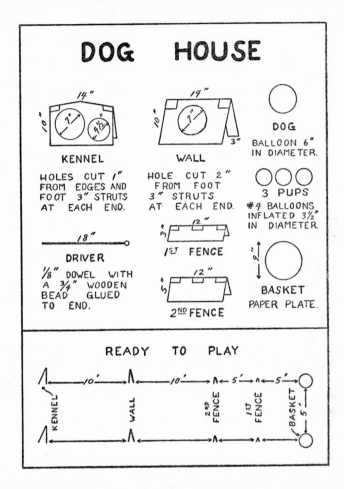

When Dog House is played as a team game, it is best to compete in relay form, with two to six players on each team. When the first player has correctly kenneled his dog and pups, he picks them up and runs back to the starting basket and puts them into it, touching off the next player. The winning team is the one which finishes first, provided each player has kenneled his canines correctly.

11.

BALL GAMES: Throwing, Tossing, Passing, Rolling, Bouncing, and Bowling Games

CIRCLE RACE BALL

FOR BOYS AND GIRLS	10 TO 20 PLAYERS	PLAYED OUTDOORS
ELEMENTARY—JR. HIGH	TEAM	OR INDOORS

An even number of players form a circle, facing inward, with 1 long pace between players. A leader stands in the middle of the circle, holding two volleyballs or basketballs, marked so that each one can be easily recognized. The players are numbered clockwise around the circle, beginning from any point of the circle. The numbers will run from 1 to the highest number of players in the circle, forming two teams with an equal number of players in each. One team is Odd and the other Even, named after the numbers borne by the players on these teams.

When each player knows his number, the leader gives a ball to Players Number 1 and Number 2. These balls have to be raced around the circle in opposite directions. Players with odd numbers toss the ball counterclockwise to other odd numbers, but in correct number sequence, 1 to 15, 15 to 13, and so on around the circle until the ball returns to Number 1 again. The even numbers pass the ball clockwise to even numbers around the circle, 2 to 4, 4 to 6, and so on. The players do not need to memorize actual numbers provided they remember that the ball must be passed to every *second* player on their right or left, as the case may be. Should a ball be dropped

166

by a player, it must be recovered by him and passed on from where he stands in the circle. A ball knocked to the ground by collision with the other ball must be retrieved by the player whose turn it was to catch, and passed on by him only after his return to his correct place in the circle.

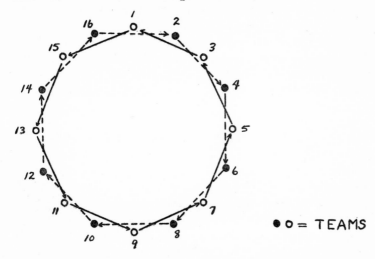

● o = TEAMS

When the leader shouts "Go!" the race begins, and the first team to complete the circle in correct sequence wins that round. The final score may be decided by the first team to finish after the ball has circled the circle three times.

A version of this game which will provide amusement for the onlookers and add difficulty and fun to the efforts of the players is played with all team members contesting blindfolded.

CIRCLE BRIDGE BALL

FOR BOYS AND GIRLS   16 TO 40 PLAYERS   PLAYED OUTDOORS
ELEMENTARY—SR. HIGH   TEAM   OR INDOORS

Two volleyballs or basketballs and a paper-plate marker 6 inches in diameter are the only equipment required for this game.

Players form two teams with the same number of players on each. Each team forms a circle with an arm's length between players. The circles should be 3 feet apart at the nearest point. All players face in the same direction around the circle and stand with the feet spread and the legs comfortably astride. The leader chooses a starting point between two players who are directly opposite each other in the circles. The paper-plate marker is placed between the circles, so that it is between these two players who will start the race. The leader gives each of them a volleyball.

The object of the game is to race the ball by rolling it on the ground under the bridges formed by the legs of the players. The ball is driven by striking it with *both* hands, and it must go around the circle three times to decide the winning team. Each player must touch the ball with both hands as it passes under him or the ball is taken back three bridges from that point as a forfeit. Each player should be ready to tap the ball forward, but not hard enough to make it pass a player or roll out of the circle, as a ball rolled out of the circle must be replaced where it left the circle and then be taken back three bridges from there as a penalty.

The first circuit of the ball is made in the direction which the players are all facing, but when the ball reaches the player who first started it rolling, he now starts the ball rolling in the opposite direction, that is, backward between the players' legs. For the third round the starter in each circle sets the ball off in the direction in which it was first rolled. The team which first gets the ball to the starter at the end of the third round is the winner.

Variations of the game may be played by having *all* players strike the ball either with the right or left hand, instead of both hands. Another amusing variation is for the leader to shout "All change!" occasionally; then the players turn around but continue to pat the ball on its way without changing its direction.

CATCH?

FOR BOYS AND GIRLS 4 TO 20 PLAYERS PLAYED OUTDOORS
ELEMENTARY—JR. HIGH INDIVIDUAL OR INDOORS

The question to be decided in this game is whether to catch or not to catch. The answer to the question lies in the skill of the leader who leads the game, though the author has seen players who could usually outguess even the most able leaders. The game certainly helps to develop alertness.

A leader has the players form a circle and number from 1 to the highest number in the circle. It is better to use the name of each player when it is known to the leader. He stands in the center of the circle holding a volleyball or some similar lightweight ball. A tennis or similar rubber ball will do, but the larger balls prove best. The players stand with their hands at their sides or, better still, held behind their backs.

The leader calls a name or number and throws or pretends to throw the ball by an underhand toss to that player. Instantly, the player whose name or number has been called must decide whether the leader is really going to throw the ball or whether he is only pretending that he will do so. Should the player decide that the leader means what he says, he brings his hands rapidly from behind his back, catches the ball, if it is thrown, and tosses it back to the leader. If a player prepares in any visible way to catch the ball and it is not thrown, that player drops out of the game, or players may be given two or three chances before being ruled out of the circle. The leader should not change his mind about a throw at the last second, and the player has so little chance to do so that he need hardly be considered from this angle.

With older players, the leader may ask all players who make the slightest motion toward catching a ball that is not thrown, to step back out of the circle. With younger participants the leader should not toss the ball much higher than the players' waists, and although the ball should be thrown immediately the name is called, it should be thrown gently.

GO BETWEEN

FOR BOYS AND GIRLS   3 TO 18 PLAYERS   PLAYED OUTDOORS
JR. HIGH—SR. HIGH   INDIVID.—TEAM

This game requires only a tennis ball, volleyball, or even a balloon weighted with a few peas inside and measuring about 8 inches in diameter, for each three players or team of players. It provides fine exercise when played as it should be —on the run.

Go Between is best played by three players or groups of three players. Two players are given a short start and pass a ball between them, at any height, as they run, keeping a distance of 6 to 10 feet between them. They may run in any direction and change direction as often as they please, provided they do not drop the ball while doing so. The third player, the catcher, tries to catch the ball at any point between the two throwers while they are in motion. The catcher must not try to snatch the ball at the moment it is thrown, nor may he tackle or touch either of the throwers. When the catcher succeeds in catching the ball, he changes places with the player who threw the ball last.

The leader decides in advance whether merely intercepting the ball without actually catching it is sufficient or if it must be caught and held by the catcher in order to score. The latter method provides better sport.

Another play-way is to have all of the other players *follow* the two throwers and try when the chance occurs to catch the ball. This makes for a rather crowded game, however, and slows it down for everybody.

As a team game, it is best played by letting two throwers from one team compete against one or more catchers from the rival team. Four throwers and two catchers, for instance, representing both teams, play at the same time, and the catcher who first catches a ball wins for his team. Throwers and catchers should take turns until everybody on each team has had a chance to both throw and catch.

As in all similar games, certain fixed boundaries covering not too much ground should be decided on before the game starts. This prevents the game from becoming a mile sprint and assures faster and better play.

CIRCLES

FOR BOYS AND GIRLS	8 TO 20 PLAYERS	PLAYED INDOORS
ELEMENTARY—JR. HIGH	INDIVID.—TEAM	OR OUTDOORS

The leader marks two circles on the ground, each 16 feet in diameter, with a distance of 6 feet between the two nearest points in the two circles. Inside each circle he draws six smaller circles, each 2 feet in diameter, as shown in the diagram. A paper-plate marker 6 inches in diameter is placed on the ground at a point halfway between the two circles. Each player stands just outside his circle with his back to the marker, and is given a well-inflated volleyball or basketball.

On the word "Go!" these two players, keeping just outside the circle, and using one hand only, start to bounce the ball clockwise around the circle. Each player may bounce the ball as often as he likes, but it must bounce, in sequence, inside *each* of the smaller circles on its way around the big circle. Should a player fail to bounce the ball in any circle, he must bounce the ball back to it and bounce it once inside the circle missed before continuing. A player who lets the ball die inside a circle must pick it up and go back a circle as a forfeit. The first player to circle the main circle correctly is the winner.

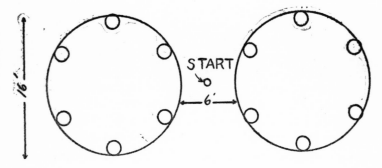

As a team relay, each team stands in line outside the main circle with the first player in line standing opposite the marker, ball in hand ready to start. After he has bounced the ball around the circle, he tosses the ball to the second player on his team and the race against the rival players in the other circle continues until each player on each team has played. The first team to finish correctly wins.

Difficulties can be added to this game by having the players bounce the ball *twice,* instead of once, in each of the smaller circles and by having players use the left hand only, or alternate hands, instead of the right hand. Interference can be introduced to cause more fun by having two players bounce balls around each circle, either as partners or rivals, one traveling clockwise and the other counterclockwise.

DARE BALL

FOR BOYS AND GIRLS   5 TO 18 PLAYERS   PLAYED OUTDOORS
ELEMENTARY—JR. HIGH   INDIVIDUAL

This fast version of Dodge Ball can be played with only a few players.

When there are only five players, four of them stand in the form of a 30-foot square. A player stands beside a marker in each corner of the square. The fifth player stands on a marker in the center of the square, armed with a not too fully inflated volleyball, which he must only throw with the left hand, unless he is a southpaw.

The game starts as the four corner players dare the ball to hit them as, any *two at a time,* they weave and dodge *diagonally* across the square while changing places. The player who throws the ball must remain on his marker and must aim below the waist level of the two runners. When a player is struck with the ball, he changes places with the thrower, or the rule may be that a player must be hit three times before he becomes the thrower.

When more than five players take part in the game, they should stand in either a large square or circle, the thrower standing as before on a marker in the center. The players try to change places with players opposite them in the square or circle, only two players moving at the same time.

Of course, the players while moving diagonally try to dodge around the ball thrower and by sudden stops and starts throw him off balance. This, combined with the left-hand-throw rule, permits many more players than might be imagined to cross safely. Players should take turns at crossing, so that all players get a fair number of tries.

CIRCLE PASS RACE

FOR BOYS AND GIRLS	16 TO 20 PLAYERS	PLAYED OUTDOORS
ELEMENTARY—JR. HIGH	TEAM	OR INDOORS

From sixteen to twenty players stand in a circle with an arm's length between players. The leader gives a volleyball or basketball to each of any two players who stand next to each other in the circle. Each becomes Number 1 player on one team. The players on the left of one Number 1 and the players on the right of the other Number 1 player count off from 2 upward, according to the number of players on each team. The players face inward toward the middle of the circle, and the two players with the highest numbers in the circle will be neighbors. The players should number off several times before the game begins so that the players will learn not only their own numbers but also where the other numbers are standing. This is good practice and proves useful in a number of games played in a similar way.

The leader gives the number order for passing each team's ball. This is how it works out for two teams of nine players in each: 1 passes to 9, 9 passes to 2, 2 to 8, 8 to 3, 3 to 7, 7 to 4, 4 to 6, 6 to 5, and 5 to 1. When a player drops a ball, it must be thrown back to the Number 1 player on that team, who throws it to the player who failed to catch it. A player who throws the ball to a wrong number on his team is penalized in the same way. These penalties slow up the speed of a team and teach the players to think fast and be careful in passing.

The first team to get the ball back to the Number 1 player is the winner of that round.

The best way to decide the winning team is to have the teams play three rounds. To keep the players on their toes and make the game more difficult, the players should be re-numbered after every third round, Number 1 becoming the highest number, and so on around each half of the circle.

DRIVE BALL

FOR BOYS AND GIRLS   6 TO 12 PLAYERS   PLAYED OUTDOORS
JR. HIGH—SR. HIGH   TEAM

Indian boys playing a somewhat similar game, on the Canadian Northwest Coast, suggested Drive Ball. The players used the inflated intestines of sea mammals, as no other balls were available. Even without the advantage of store-bought balls, these Indian players had developed considerable skill and good throwing judgment, which should encourage better-equipped players to do still better.

In this amusing and exciting game a certain combination of skill of hands and eyes decides the winning team. One white and two brown volleyballs, basketballs, or soccer balls are needed for each team of three players. The difference in color is essential to distinguish between the two balls which are thrown and the one which is driven. Colored-paper circles pasted onto the balls will serve quite well when only balls of one color are available. In addition to the three balls required for each team, eight paper-plate markers 6 inches in diameter are required for markers. One marker is painted yellow, another red, and the other six remain white. The last requirement is eight wire staples to fasten the markers to the ground. How to make and use these staples is described in Chapter 3.

A circle 30 feet in diameter is marked on the ground. On one side of it a red marker is stapled, and directly across the circle, opposite the red marker, the yellow marker is stapled. Three markers are stapled on each of the other two sides of the circle, one of these plates being directly in the middle of each side of the circle, as shown in the diagram. The game is now set up and the teams can take positions.

A team of three players lines up 1 foot away from and directly in front of the yellow marker, toward which their backs are turned. The rival team of three players stands in a similar position, directly on the other side of the yellow marker and facing away from it. The two outside players on each team are each given a brown ball. Directly in front of each team and 1 short pace away, a white ball is placed on the ground.

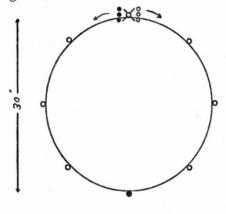

X = YELLOW MARKER
● = RED MARKER
○ = WHITE MARKERS
⬤○
⬤○ = TEAMS

On the word "Play!" the players on each team throw the two brown balls, always from between waist and chin level, at the white ball, trying to drive it around the circle as quickly as possible but so that it touches each marker, except the marker at the beginning of the race. Each team plays in any formation that it wishes throughout the game. The first team to touch the yellow marker at the starting point with the white ball is the winner, provided it has followed these simple rules. The use of feet is barred, and any player who uses one or both feet to propel or stop a ball causes his team to be sent back one marker as a penalty. A player should pass the ball after three throws, unless it bounces directly back into his hands on rebound from the white ball or the ground. Whichever of the three players on a team is nearest to a brown ball either picks the brown ball up and throws it at the white ball or throws it to a teammate who is in a better position to use it to advantage. When a marker is bypassed on the way around the circle, the white ball must be driven back and the missed marker hit before the team proceeds to the next marker. A player must not intentionally throw either of his team's throwing balls at any ball of the opposing team. Should a player do so, his team must drive its white ball back one marker as a penalty.

Suspense and excitement occur when the two teams meet close to or at one of the markers.

Another way to dispute this match is for the leader to give each team only one brown throwing ball, instead of two.

Another amusing way to play Drive Ball is to have both teams start from the yellow marker, facing in the same direction and traveling in the same direction around the circle. This version causes plently of congestion at each marker; despite this, a team which plays skillfully can beat the other team and still make good time around the circle.

With more than six players, the game is best played in two circles with a distance of 12 feet between the circles.

DODGE BALL DUEL

FOR BOYS AND GIRLS	10 TO 30 PLAYERS	PLAYED OUTDOORS
ELEMENTARY—JR. HIGH	INDIVIDUAL	OR INDOORS

The players stand in a circle, about 40 feet in diameter or more, for this game which requires only a volleyball, or similar ball, not fully inflated, as equipment. The players face inward toward the center of the circle. If the leader does not know the names of all of the players he can number them, being careful to call two names or numbers which are as far apart in the circle as possible, so that players will have to run from different parts of the circle.

The leader stands in the center of the circle and throws a volleyball as high and as straight up into the air as possible.

He calls out two names or two numbers while the ball is high in air. The players whose names are called run into the circle and each tries to catch the ball before it hits the ground. The player who catches the ball stands on the spot where he made the catch. From there, he throws the ball at the player who missed the catch, trying to hit him before he gets back to his correct place in the circle.

A player hit by the ball is out of the game, as is a player who runs into a wrong place in the circle. The thrower who misses his mark is also ruled out of the game.

As many players as possible should be called during a game so that the majority of the players will have an opportunity to catch or throw.

HAND TO HAND

FOR BOYS AND GIRLS	4 TO 8 PLAYERS	PLAYED OUTDOORS
ELEMENTARY—JR. HIGH	INDIVIDUAL	OR INDOORS

This is an easy feat to perform by one's self but it is another matter when competing with another player in an effort to combine style and speed. The two players who are contesting stand opposite and facing each other about 4 feet apart. Each player is given a soft rubber ball similar in size to a tennis ball, or a tennis ball if available, but each player must have the same sort of ball.

When the leader says "Go!" each player begins to pass the ball from hand to hand with the hands held just above waist level, bouncing it fairly fast from one hand to the other and making it always travel the width of the body between hands. Players may begin fairly slowly and gradually increase speed until one player misses the ball, leaving the other the winner. The winner of one pair competes against another winner, and so it continues until a champion is discovered. The leader may have to decide who is the winner when a pair of boys who are almost equally good are contesting. Then speed, style, the length the ball travels between hands, and the fact that hands are held in a horizontal line are the deciding factors in naming the winner.

THREE TIMES ROUND

FOR BOYS AND GIRLS   4 TO 10 PLAYERS   PLAYED INDOORS
ELEMENTARY—JR. HIGH   INDIVID.—TEAM   OR OUTDOORS

The players stand in a circle or square with 3 feet clearance on all sides of each player. The leader gives each player a tennis ball or another good bouncing ball of the same size. The game is played by bouncing a ball in a complete circle without changing places except for turning around as the ball is bounced from waist high onto the ground. The players turn around to the right for the first circle, bouncing the ball with the right hand only. For the second circle, the turn is made toward the left and the ball is bounced with the left hand only. The third and last circle is made by turning around to the right and bouncing the ball with the right and left hand alternately. The ball must always be bounced directly in front of or between the feet and not to one side or the other. The first player to complete the triple circle correctly is the winner. When a ball is fumbled or bounced too far away to be re-bounced without taking a step in some direction, the player may be ruled out of the game or given another chance, in which case he must begin the round again from the starting point of the circle.

When played as a team game, the same number of players are assigned to each team and all teams start to circle when the leader calls "Go!" The team whose players circle in correct sequence and finish first wins.

NUMBERS UP!

FOR BOYS AND GIRLS   10 TO 30 PLAYERS   PLAYED OUTDOORS
ELEMENTARY—JR. HIGH   INDIVIDUAL   OR INDOORS

The players stand in a big circle, facing inward toward the center of the circle, and number off from 1 to the highest number in the circle. There should be a distance of an arm's length between players. A paper-plate marker is placed directly in the center of the circle. One player stands on the marker, armed with a rather soft volleyball. He calls out any two numbers held by players in the circle—using most frequently numbers such as 1 and 15, 7 and 19, and other numbers which cause the players to run almost across the circle to exchange places. The two players whose numbers are called must immediately change places. The player with the ball tries to hit either of these players while they are running between places. He must aim below the waist and should not throw the ball too hard. A player who is struck below the waist by the ball is out of the game. A leader may keep the same player in the center of the circle for as long a period as he wishes, and he may replace him at any time by putting the player who is missed by the thrower's ball into the center position.

POT SHOTS

FOR BOYS AND GIRLS	2 TO 14 PLAYERS	PLAYED OUTDOORS
ELEMENTARY—JR. HIGH	INDIVID.—TEAM	OR INDOORS

A tennis ball or any soft rubber ball about the same size is needed for each team. Two lines are marked on the ground 30 feet apart, while a third line is marked on the ground halfway between these two lines and parallel to them. The leader places three paper, cone-shaped drinking cups, 18 inches apart, on the center line.

A team of two to seven players lines up behind each of the end lines and a ball is given to each team. On the word "Throw!" the player with the ball on each team throws at any one of the cups, trying to knock it over. Cups must actually be knocked over, not just moved out of place. Players should take turns at throwing the balls so that all have a fair chance to score. A player may only score one cup with one shot even if two cups are knocked over with one throw. The second cup is replaced on the line. Each cup knocked down counts 5 points, and the game continues until all three cups have been hit.

When the players prove to be good shots, six cups instead of three may be set up as targets. In order to still further reduce cup casualties, only one ball may be used between two teams, each team throwing at the cups in turn.

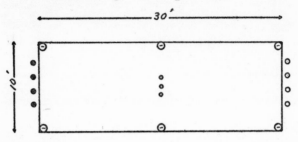

⊙ = MARKERS
o = CUPS
•o = TEAMS

Still another good way to play Pot Shots is to use volleyballs or basketballs instead of the smaller balls, the larger balls being thrown with *both* hands either from above the head or from waist level, as decided by the leader. In case of ties between teams in this version of the game, a second game may be played with the ball being thrown with only one hand instead of two.

CIRCLE BALL

FOR BOYS AND GIRLS   8 TO 20 PLAYERS   PLAYED INDOORS
JR. HIGH—SR. HIGH   INDIVIDUAL   OR OUTDOORS

This is a favorite game in Japan. When played outdoors it requires a smooth, even surface. The players stand about 2 feet apart in a circle, facing inward toward the center of the circle. The leader gives a tennis ball or a similar rubber ball which bounces well to any player in the circle. Should no small ball be available, the game can be played with a well-inflated volleyball.

The player with the ball immediately begins to bounce it on the floor in front of him, hitting it with the open palm of one hand only. He bounces the ball as often as possible, trying to keep it within easy reach, since he must not move his feet. When the ball escapes beyond reach, the player nearest to it takes over and continues to keep it bouncing. When a player misses the ball or allows it to stop bouncing, he leaves the circle. The game stops for a moment, the circle closes in a little, and then the game starts again.

CIRCLE BOUNCE BALL

| FOR BOYS AND GIRLS | 3 TO 10 PLAYERS | PLAYED INDOORS |
| JR. HIGH—SR. HIGH | INDIVIDUAL | OR OUTDOORS |

In this game, each player bounces a tennis or similar ball, with good bounce, completely around a circle in the following manner. A circle measuring about 9 feet in diameter is marked on the floor. A chalked cross just outside any part of the circle indicates the starting point. From there, a player advances at a walking pace, around and just inside the circle, bouncing the ball with one hand, the same one throughout the game, as close to the circle outline as possible at all times, until he has circled the circle. He faces around the circle as he moves constantly forward and he must not step more than a foot away from the circle outline. Should the ball bounce beyond his reach, he is out of the game.

The leader may vary this game by having players bounce the ball with alternate hands and while circling the circle backward.

BULL'S EYE

| FOR BOYS AND GIRLS | 2 TO 12 PLAYERS | PLAYED OUTDOORS |
| ELEMENTARY | INDIVIDUAL | OR INDOORS |

This is one of a series of games all of which require the same equipment. The leader can make a rope circle by tying the two ends of a 5-foot length of rope together, or a wooden or metal hoop about 18 inches in diameter will make even a better circle. A volleyball, basketball, or tennis ball is required for each group of players. The circle is placed on the ground in the middle of a circle which is marked on the ground and has a diameter of 20 or 30 feet.

The players stand just outside of the big circle. The leader throws any player a ball and he tries to bounce it inside the hoop by an underhand toss, released when the hands are at head level. If the ball lands inside the hoop, it scores 5 points and the player is given another throw, but not more than two throws in succession. The winning score for the game may be counted as 20 or 30.

Variety may be introduced into this and the following game by letting the players bounce the ball from an over-the-head position, instead of using the underhand toss.

BOUNCE OUT, BOUNCE IN

FOR BOYS AND GIRLS	2 TO 12 PLAYERS	PLAYED OUTDOORS
ELEMENTARY	INDIVIDUAL	OR INDOORS

This is a more difficult way of playing the preceding game of Bull's Eye. Using the underhand toss, each player takes turns at trying to bounce the ball once outside the hoop before it bounces inside the hoop. The ball must bounce inside the hoop on the second bounce or it does not score. A ball bouncing inside on the second bounce scores 5 points, and the player is given a second try, but not a third, even if he scores the second time as well as the first. The total score for this game may be counted as 20 or 30.

TARGET BOUNCE BALL

FOR BOYS AND GIRLS	8 TO 20 PLAYERS	PLAYED OUTDOORS
ELEMENTARY—JR. HIGH	TEAM	OR INDOORS

Two teams with four to ten players on each side stand evenly spaced and facing each other across a 30-foot circle. Each team has one half of the circle, in the middle of which a target circle 18 inches in diameter has been plainly marked. The only equipment needed is two well-inflated volleyballs or basketballs, one being given to each team.

On the word "Go!" one player on each team tries to bounce the ball, from above head level, on the target so that the ball continues on to the opposing team on the other side of the

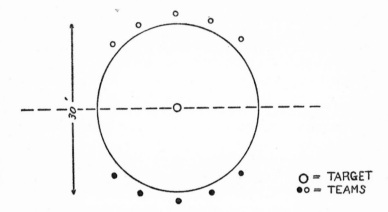

O = TARGET
●o = TEAMS

circle. Players who miss the target three times are ruled out of the game, and all players who miss or drop possible catches after the ball has bounced from the target or target area are also out of the game. No player on either team should throw the ball twice in succession, and the ball should be passed from player to player so that all have an equal number of throws. Each strike on the target can count 5 points, or the winning team can be the one which has the most players in action after five minutes of play.

This game can be made harder or easier by reducing the size of the target or making the circle larger, or making the target larger or reducing the size of the circle.

12.

BALL GAMES: Dribbling and Kicking Games

DIAMOND SOCCER

FOR BOYS	4 TO 12 PLAYERS	PLAYED OUTDOORS
ELEMENTARY—JR. HIGH	INDIVID.—TEAM	OR INDOORS

For this game, six white paper-plate markers 6 inches in diameter and a volleyball, basketball, or soccer ball are needed for each player or team. Four plate markers are stapled to the ground in a diamond pattern 12 feet apart, as shown in the diagram. A ball is placed on each starting marker, situated in front of one end of the diamond, as illustrated. A player or team stands behind each ball, facing the markers.

On the word "Kick!" each player starts to dribble his ball as fast as he can completely around each of the markers, but avoiding the nearest marker until the return trip. The player on the right works in a counterclockwise direction, while the one on the left dribbles in a clockwise direction. The ball must not touch any of the markers, though it may be dribbled as close to them as a player dares. Should a ball touch a marker, it must be dribbled back one marker as a penalty, and the game continued from there. To finish the race, the ball must be dribbled back onto the starting marker. Hands must not be used at any time. The interference which the players may meet as they encounter each other at a marker adds spice to the game.

When Diamond Soccer is played as a team game, teams of two partner-players start from the starting markers. The part-

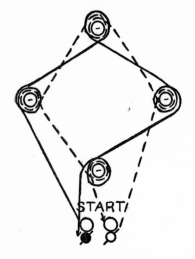

⊖ = MARKERS

⌀⌀ = PLAYERS

ners dribble the ball from one to another, circling the markers as fast as possible without touching them with the ball.

Another form of this game is a team relay match which is played with two to six players on each team. The players on both teams can either play one at a time, each player touching off the next when the circuit is completed, or team members can play as partners, which, of course, requires an even number of players on each team. Teammate partners also play in relay fashion.

DRIBBLE BALL

FOR BOYS	10 TO 20 PLAYERS	PLAYED OUTDOORS
ELEMENTARY—SR. HIGH	INDIVID.—PARTNER	OR INDOORS

The players stand in a circle, all facing around it in the same direction, with 3 feet between players. A paper-plate marker 6 inches in diameter is stapled to the ground just outside the circle and between any two players. This marks the starting point of the race. The two players stand back to back beside the marker, and the leader gives each one a volleyball or basketball.

On the word "Kick!" each player dribbles the ball in soccer fashion between and around all of the players in the circle. The players who dribble the balls must do the best they can when they meet, as they are sure to do, at some point on their way around the circle and back to the starting point. There is no rule regarding the distance at which players in the circle must be circled by the dribbled ball but it must go completely around each player as it is woven around the circle. The ball which first touches the marker after the circuit has been completed decides the winner, and two other players take over.

An exciting and none-too-easy partner-team race may be carried out by having two teams with two players in each dribble the ball from one to another around the players in the circle, as described above. Two player-partners weave their way clockwise around the circle, while the other two players dribble their ball in a counterclockwise direction.

Dribble Ball also makes a good relay race, with the players in the circle divided into two teams of equal size. The teams move around the circle in opposite directions, the players dribbling singly and touching off the next player after circling the circle, until each member of both teams has made the circuit.

As good dribbling is really scientific and dribbling a ball *around* each player may prove a little too difficult for the average player, this game can be greatly simplified in all of its versions by having the individual players or teams simply dribble the ball *between* each pair of players, instead of *around* each player.

SOCCER DRIVE BALL

FOR BOYS   6 TO 12 PLAYERS   PLAYED OUTDOORS
JR. HIGH—SR. HIGH   TEAM

This game is played in the same way as Drive Ball, in the preceding chapter, with an important difference—it is played with the feet. There are three players on each team, as before, but only one brown ball is used to drive the white ball forward to the various markers. The white and brown balls, one of each color or identified by color patches if the balls are the same color, should both be fully inflated. Eight white paper-plate markers 6 inches in diameter—one colored red, one colored yellow, and the other six white—complete the equipment required. The diagram showing the layout for Drive Ball gives the positions for players and markers around the edge of the 30-foot-in-diameter circle. In shows that the two teams play around the circle in opposite directions, starting from the yellow marker and finishing the game at the same point. Difficulty will arise as the rival teams reach a marker at the same time, but this adds to the fun. The use of hands is barred in this game and a player who touches the ball, even unintentionally, with a hand or hands causes his team to be told to dribble their brown ball back one marker as a penalty. When a player, in the excitement of the game, kicks his team's white ball in error, it must be replaced in the same position in which it was before being kicked, and the team must dribble its brown ball back one marker before dribbling on to the white ball again. All markers must be touched by the white ball in passing; when a marker is missed, the team must dribble the brown ball against the white ball until it is in position for a second try.

The three players on each team must work out a strategy so that the kicked ball does not hit the white ball too forcibly as it is driven against it because, in the case of a miss, the brown ball will overshoot the mark too far and slow down the game while it is being dribbled back into position for another try. The players must also decide when a pass to a teammate is better than kicking the ball themselves. With a little practice in dribbling and passing, a team can develop skill.

NINEPINS BALL

FOR BOYS AND GIRLS   2 TO 10 PLAYERS   PLAYED INDOORS
ELEMENTARY—JR. HIGH   INDIVID.—TEAM   OR OUTDOORS

The only gear needed for this game is six cone-shaped paper drinking cups, six paper-plate markers 6 inches in diameter, and one tennis ball or soft rubber ball of about the same size. A line is marked on the floor and the six cups are placed, point upward and 12 inches apart, on the center part of the line. A kickoff line, 20 feet distant from the center line, is drawn directly opposite it and parallel with it toward each end of this play area. When only two players or teams take part, one ball is used.

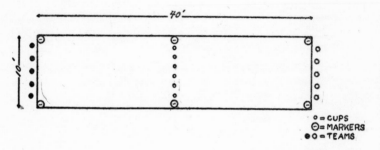

To begin play, a player at one end kicks off in an attempt to knock over as many cups as possible. It proves difficult to hit even one of them, since kicking the ball straight enough to connect with the cups is no easy task. The ball is now kicked from the other end by a player or team member, and the game continues until all of the cups have been knocked over or driven at least 12 inches away from the center line. In team play, each team should take turns at kicking the ball, and every member on the team should get turns at kicking. As each cup is knocked out, it is taken from the line by the leader. The player or team which knocks out the most cups in the shortest time is the winner. In the second game, the end which kicked first in the first game kicks off second.

An exciting and surprising variation of this game is to play it with a volleyball or basketball. Usually the players express their surprise when one of these balls is introduced into the game. Their astonishment increases when they discover that the much bigger ball does almost as little damage as the smaller ball.

As the players become more skillful, the distance between the kickoff lines and the row of cups can be increased, and the cups can also be placed farther apart.

As all soccer players know, it is difficult to kick a ball in a straight line by using the point of the shoe. The ball may, with a little practice, be driven in a straighter line by striking it with either side of the ball of the foot.

CROQUET SOCCER

FOR BOYS	10 TO 30 PLAYERS	PLAYED OUTDOORS
ELEMENTARY—SR. HIGH	INDIVID.—TEAM	OR INDOORS

This is a tricky game in which only good footwork will take a team of two players back to the starting marker in quick time. The only gear required is two soccer balls, volleyballs, or basketballs and a paper-plate marker 6 inches in diameter. All the players except four stand in a circle about 3 feet apart. Naturally, the greater the number of players, the larger the circle. When there are few players, they should stand farther apart in order to assure a circle of about 30 feet in diameter. The players number from 1 to the highest number in the circle. The odd numbers face around the ring in one direction, while the even numbers face inward toward the center of the circle. They all stand with legs in an easy feet-astride position, the legs not too far apart yet not too close. A paper-plate marker is placed just inside the circle between players 1 and 2. The four players, not in the circle, form teams of twos, facing each other across the marker, one teammate inside and one outside the circle. The leader gives each team a ball.

On the word "Go!" each team kicks the ball from teammate

to teammate between the legs of each player in the circle, each team working in an opposite direction. Balls which strike a leg and bounce out of or into the circle must be retrieved by kicking and then driven between the pair of legs which was missed, before the players go on to the next pair. The first team to circle the circle correctly and arrive back at the starting marker is the winner. Fun and additional hazard enter the game when opposing teams clash on the way around the circle.

SOCCER HOOP BALL

FOR BOYS	4 TO 12 PLAYERS	PLAYED OUTDOORS
ELEMENTARY—JR. HIGH	INDIVID.—TEAM	OR INDOORS

While watching some champion Scottish soccer players kick soccer balls through small hoops, with amazing accuracy and at equally amazing range, Soccer Hoop Ball, with some of the virtuosity kicked out, was born.

This is another game where those who play soccer may have the edge on the other players, though it does not always work out that way. All that is required in the way of equipment is a wooden or metal hoop about 18 inches in diameter and an inch or so wide, and two or three volleyballs or basketballs.

The leader distributes the balls among the players who stand in a circle about 40 feet in diameter with the hoop directly in its center. The players take turns in trying to kick the balls so that they will roll inside the hoop and stay there. No player should kick a ball twice in succession, so that all may have an equal chance to score. Two or more balls may be kicked at the same time, so the leader will have to keep an eye open in order to see which ball scores. A ball which goes inside the hoop and remains there scores 5 points. A ball which rolls in but rolls out again only scores 3 points. A ball knocked out of the hoop by another ball does not score, nor does the player whose ball knocked it out score, though such kicks cause fun and uncertainty in the final score. The winner is the player who first gets three balls, kicked during one game, into the hoop.

This is a good contest with two teams of three to six players on each. Each team stands on one side of the circle and each team is given a ball. They may take turns at kicking or the leader may decide that they shoot at will. The rules are the same as for individual play, and the first team to score three times into the hoop wins.

This game may also be played with tennis balls or any small rubber balls when larger ones are not available.

CIRCLE BRIDGE KICK

FOR BOYS AND GIRLS   20 TO 30 PLAYERS   PLAYED OUTDOORS
ELEMENTARY—SR. HIGH   INDIVIDUAL   OR INDOORS

The players form a circle, at least 20 feet in diameter, facing its center, with their feet an easy pace apart. The outside of each player's foot touches the foot of the player on either side of him. One player stands in the middle of the circle. The leader gives him a volleyball or similar lightweight ball, not too fully inflated, which the player in the center tries to kick, not too forcibly, along the ground between the legs of any player in the circle. If the player chosen cannot keep the ball on the ground, he should speedily be replaced by a player who can. The players in the circle place their hands on their knees and try to stop the ball with their hands before it rolls between their legs. The player should only lower his hands when he sees the ball coming directly toward him. The hands may also be used to stop the ball at any time if it should rise from the ground and threaten to strike a player on the body or face.

All balls which are stopped are kicked back to the player in the middle of the circle. He should kick the ball toward a different part of the circle each time. The center man fields all balls which are poorly returned to him and, if he judges it necessary, the leader can have a fielder or two outside the circle to retrieve balls which go outside the ring of players.

Such fielding prevents the breaking and re-forming of the circle, which happens when players forming the circle field the ball.

When the ball passes between a player's legs, he drops out of the game and the other players close in a little to tighten the circle. The leader may choose a new center player after three players have been put out of the game, or at any other time.

The game continues until the circle has been so reduced in size that there are not a sufficient number of players left to form a worth-while circle. Of course, as the circle becomes smaller, the ball is kicked less forcibly and the player who kicks it will be more successful if he whirls and kicks in an unexpected direction.

BALL HOP RACE

FOR BOYS AND GIRLS   2 TO 10 PLAYERS   PLAYED OUTDOORS
ELEMENTARY—JR. HIGH   INDIVID.—TEAM   OR INDOORS

Six white paper-plate markers 9 inches in diameter are placed on the ground in a 20-foot circle, as shown in the diagram, and a seventh plate is placed directly in the center of the others as the finishing point of the race. A volleyball or basketball is placed beside each starting marker, and two players at a time contest.

On the word "Go!" each player, while hopping on one foot, drives his ball around each one of the markers, in any order, so long as the ball is kicked completely around each marker and back to the starting point. A player whose ball hits a marker can either be ruled out of the game or be sent back one marker as a penalty. When a player has circled all of the markers, he must kick the ball into the center plate so that it stays there, in order to win.

As a team game, it is played in relay form with two to five players on each team. When one player has completed the course, the next player starts, but he must hop-kick the ball back to the starting point before starting to circle the markers.

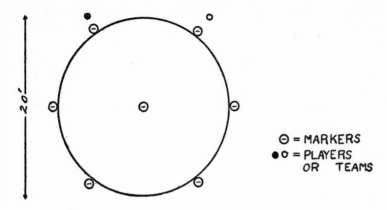

⊖ = MARKERS
●○ = PLAYERS
OR TEAMS

The first team whose players circle all markers correctly, not forgetting to kick the ball into the center plate each time, is the winner.

SOCCER GOLF

FOR BOYS AND GIRLS   2 TO 10 PLAYERS   PLAYED OUTDOORS
ELEMENTARY—JR. HIGH   INDIVID.—TEAM   OR INDOORS

Six empty tin cans, about the size of large evaporated milk cans, are placed in a circle 5 feet apart. These serve as targets, and two volleyballs or similar large balls complete the required equipment.

One player is given a ball and he starts 6 feet outside the circle, at any point. He starts to kick the ball from there around the circle, in either direction, knocking down as many cans in as few kicks as possible on the way around to the starting point again. He may kick at any can in any order but not more than one can may be knocked over at a time. The players take turns, and the one who knocks over, not just displaces, all of the cans in the fewest kicks is the winner.

Soccer Golf can also be played by two players, each kicking the same sort of ball in opposite directions around the circle, from the starting point back to the starting point. The player hitting the greatest number of cans on the way is the winner.

Of course, there may be complications as the players meet on their way around the circle, but that makes the game more fun.

Another version of this game is for teams of two players in each to contest their way, in opposite directions, around the circle. Smart dribbling and passing will help a team to go around the circuit in quick time, knocking out the targets en route.

DAISY CUTTER

FOR BOYS AND GIRLS	4 TO 14 PLAYERS	PLAYED OUTDOORS
ELEMENTARY—SR. HIGH	INDIVIDUAL	OR INDOORS

This game provides fun as well as fine practice for players who wish to develop real skill in kicking. Little equipment is required and it may be used again and again. Two poles about 1 inch thick and 5 feet long, a longer pole from 8 to 10 feet long and 1 to 2 inches in diameter, and a soccer ball, volleyball, or basketball complete the gear needed. The two short poles are driven 1 foot into the ground, 8 feet apart, then lines are marked with chalk or crayon on each pole, facing the kickoff line, 20 feet distant. The first mark on each pole should be 12 inches above ground level, and four more marks are made 6 inches apart on each pole, the top one being at a height of 3 feet above ground level.

The players line up behind the kickoff line with the exception of two who hold the long pole against the two uprights, one player at either end, starting at the top marks and working downward, on the direction of the leader. The players at the kickoff line take turns at kicking the ball, which is placed on the ground just in front of that line. The object of the game is for each player to try and drive the ball with one kick, from the kickoff point, under the bar and, of course, between the two uprights forming the miniature goal posts. The leader in charge may decide to let each player take a kick with the bar at the top height or he may let a player take another try each time he kicks the ball below the bar. The horizontal bar is lowered one mark, 6 inches, on either side after each player has had his turn at kicking the ball with the bar at the former level.

The winner is the player who first kicks the ball three times below the bar when it has been lowered to the 12-inch level.

Many players are surprised to find how difficult it is to drive the ball straight forward on ground level. For old hands, the leader may add the considerable handicap of asking the players to kick off with a drop kick, the ball being dropped with one or two hands before being kicked toward the goal. Another way to make this game more difficult is to increase the distance from which the kickoff is made or to lower the marks on the foot of the uprights to 11 inches above ground level, which only leaves a clearance margin of roughly 1½ inches, for the basketball, instead of 2½ inches. The player who can drive the ball under the bar held at minimum clearance height is certainly a "Daisy Cutter."

FORWARD?

FOR BOYS	4 TO 12 PLAYERS	PLAYED OUTDOORS
ELEMENTARY—JR. HIGH	INDIVIDUAL	OR INDOORS

The question is how many of the players will actually go *forward* in this blindfold dribbling skill test? The equipment required for this game is a soccer ball, volleyball, or basketball for each player. Two lines 40 feet apart and 30 feet long are marked on the ground opposite each other.

The players line up 6 feet apart on the starting line. Each player is then blindfolded and given a ball. On the word "Forward!" each player places the ball on the ground directly in front of him and dribbles it from foot to foot, if he knows how to dribble, or in some other fashion if he doesn't, in as straight a line as possible toward the finishing line. The winner is the player who is *closest* to his ball when he dribbles it across any part of the finish line. This rule is to prevent a player from kicking the ball 10 to 20 feet ahead of him when he feels that he is nearing the finishing mark. All players must stop immediately on one blast of the leader's whistle, blown to prevent collision between any two players.

This game is fun to watch, since few, if any, players travel in a straight line. Some are quite likely to circle and finish at the point from which they started. This sort of finish happens more frequently when the lines can be marked farther apart, say 50 or 60 feet instead of 40.

The spectators on the side lines and elsewhere should be asked not to talk or make any noise during this contest, because doing so helps inform the players of the direction in which they are traveling. The leader can introduce an additional hazard for senior players by telling each player quietly, or touching him on the shoulder, when he has arrived at the finish line. The player then turns around and dribbles the ball back to the starting point, where the winner is decided.

13.

Balloon Games

How to prepare balloons. Toy balloon inflation and tying present technical difficulties which are not always appreciated by novice leaders.

Fastening the necks of balloons so that they retain the air throughout play periods presents no problems when one of the three following methods is used. Strong, fairly heavy wool may be used to tie the necks of balloons after they are blown up. If a clove hitch knot is used, this method is doubly sure-fire. Another good way to get a balloon ready in a hurry, with the certainty that it will not deflate, is to wind a very small rubber band around the neck a number of times. The best method of all, for use on small balloons which may be used time and again for many games without deflating, is to inflate the balloon fairly fully and then tie a single knot in the neck. The very end of the neck is held in the fingers of one hand after the knot is made and the balloon is pulled gently but firmly away from the end of the neck by pulling gently on the knot. The end of the neck is then snipped off and the balloon is round and ready for action.

Care should be taken when ordering balloons to specify *round* ones, since the long and pear-shaped balloons are of little use for games. Round balloons Numbers 4 and 5 are good for many games where the balloons are propelled with wands or blown along the ground. A balloon which is almost blown up to the maximum possible size will usually burst when exposed to the hot sun for a while. Such a balloon will also burst very easily when crushed a little or struck too forcibly. New balloons should be inflated fairly fully the day before they are going to be used, left inflated overnight, and the necks untied next day so that the air escapes. Balloons treated in this way will inflate much more easily and be considerably larger when blown up again before the games are played. A partially inflated balloon is much stronger than a fully inflated one and will take far more punishment during games in which they are used roughly. The safety margin should be small though, as players get less fun from playing with balloons which are not firm enough to bounce well or respond quickly to a sharp tap with the hand.

In playing balloon games when a light breeze is blowing, it is best to put two or three whole, dried peas into the balloon before inflating it. The peas act as ballast and help to keep the balloon from blowing about too easily. The peas inside the balloon also cause it to come down faster when it is thrown or bumped into the air. This is a slight advantage for the players in some games and a slight handicap in others.

VARIETY BALLOON CONTEST

FOR BOYS AND GIRLS   2 TO 12 PLAYERS   PLAYED OUTDOORS
ELEMENTARY—JR. HIGH   INDIVID.—TEAM   OR INDOORS

When this game is played by two players, they bounce a balloon to each other over two markers. For six players, three markers are placed on the ground in a straight line, 3 feet apart. The other three markers are put directly opposite them, also in line, with a distance of 4 feet between the two lines. A balloon which should measure 8 or 10 inches in diameter when inflated is required for each two players or two teams.

The opposing players stand facing each other on opposite sides of the markers. One player tosses the balloon up and bounces it high over the markers to the other player. Each player makes the first three serves with the palm of the *right* hand only. Only one stroke is allowed for each serve and if the balloon falls between the markers, it is considered out of play and is thrown up again by the player who made the faulty serve, in order to continue the game. Each player makes the second three serves with the palm of the *left* hand; the third three serves with the *back* of the *right* hand; and the fourth, and last, three serves with the *back* of the *left* hand. A player who makes two faulty serves in succession loses the game, as does the player who allows the balloon to fall three times in his territory, which is close to his marker or anywhere behind or to one side of it. Should both players still be in the game at the end of the fourth series of serves, the game may be started again, as before, and played until one player is the winner.

When this game is played by teams, there should be two players on each team. They stand side by side, facing their two opponents. One balloon will be needed for each two opposing teams and it is best to use balloons of different colors when several teams are playing, so that opposing teams know their balloon. The rules for team play are the same as for individual players, though the leader may change the number of serves in each series if he wishes.

BALLOON KICK RACE

FOR BOYS AND GIRLS	2 TO 12 PLAYERS	PLAYED OUTDOORS
ELEMENTARY—JR. HIGH	INDIVID.—TEAM	OR INDOORS

When this game is played outdoors on a day when a slight breeze is blowing, each balloon requires two or three whole, dried peas in it so that it will not blow about too easily. A balloon, inflated to about 6 inches, is required for each player or team, and also three white paper saucers 5 inches in diameter. A starting line is marked on the ground, 3 feet in front of the first row of saucers, as shown in the drawing. The three saucers are placed 15 feet apart in a straight line, beginning three feet from the starting line. The lanes between the rows of saucers should be 3 feet apart.

For individual play, a balloon is given to each player as he stands just behind the starting line. On the word "Kick!" each player kicks his balloon down his line of saucers, kicking it into each saucer for a moment on the way to the last one.

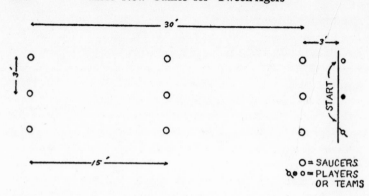

O = SAUCERS
⦾ o = PLAYERS
OR TEAMS

Players must actually put the balloon into each saucer, not just touch it in passing or kick it so that it rolls over the saucer.

When older players compete, the race should continue back from the second line to the starting point. On the return trip the players must hop on one foot, kicking the balloon with the other foot. The first player to reach the finish line, provided he has played the game correctly, is the winner.

In an amusing version, teams of two players kick and dribble the balloon to each other, observing the same rules as given above. Balloon Kick Race also makes a good relay.

BALLOON HOOP BOUNCE

FOR BOYS AND GIRLS   2 TO 12 PLAYERS   PLAYED OUTDOORS
ELEMENTARY—JR. HIGH   INDIVID.—TEAM   OR INDOORS

For this game, a balloon inflated to 6 or 8 inches and a wooden hoop 18 inches in diameter are required for each two players or two teams of two or three players on each team. A player is also needed to hold each hoop; he gets a close-up of the game and the chance of playing in the next one. When playing Hoop Bounce indoors, however, the hoops may be suspended from the ceiling.

Two lines are marked on the ground opposite each other and 10 feet apart, while another line is marked in the center directly between these two lines. Individual players or teams stand facing each other immediately behind the outside lines. The player holding the hoop stands in the middle of the center line. He should hold the hoop out in one hand with arm outstretched and the bottom of the hoop at shoulder level. The opening in the hoop faces the two lines, and the players should stand as directly opposite it as possible.

The leader gives one player the inflated balloon and on the word "Go!" that player, keeping behind the line, bounces the balloon through the hoop with an underhand pat, using only one hand, to the player on the other side. The balloon must reach the line opposite the one from which it has been driven or 2 points are deducted from the score of the player or team whose drive fell short. The players continue to drive the balloon back and forward through the hoop, always remaining behind the line, where they stand until a player lets the balloon fall to the ground, misses the hoop, or hits the rim of the hoop so that the balloon is out of play. The player or team doing so loses 5 points for each of these faults. The game may be decided by considering the player or team first losing 15 or 20 points as the loser. The distance between the players and the hoop can be lengthened or shortened according to the skill of the players, and two or three round, dried peas may be put inside the balloon to add a little weight and increase the distance it will travel.

When teams are competing, each one stands behind its line, and the players on the team either take turns or co-operate in driving the balloon through the hoop to the other team.

When ties between evenly matched teams or players have to be decided, the leader may ask all players to use only the left hand throughout the tie-breaking game.

A larger hoop, up to 24 inches in diameter, may be used for younger players or to afford older players on teams a better chance to make angle drives.

BALLOON DRIVE

FOR BOYS AND GIRLS   2 TO 12 PLAYERS   PLAYED OUTDOORS
ELEMENTARY   INDIVID.—TEAM

This is a balloon race for which the only equipment is a balloon about 8 inches in diameter when inflated, for each player. Two lines are marked on the ground opposite each other 30 feet apart. Two paper-plate markers can be used for each two players, to take the place of the lines. The players line up behind the starting point, holding the balloons.

On the word "Go!" the players race for the second line, driving the balloons forward with sharp pats with the palm of the *right* hand only, without letting them fall to the ground. If a player drops a balloon, he must pick it up, step back 3 paces, and continue from there. On reaching the second line, the players turn and without stopping or holding the balloons, they drive them back to the starting point, using the *left* hand only for the return run.

When played as a team game the teams are evenly divided in two; two or more players line up behind each other in each half of the team. Each half-team stands directly opposite the other behind the two lines. On the word "Go!" the first player on each team races from the starting point, driving the balloon with the *right* hand only to the player on the opposite line. That player returns it, batting it forward, with the *left* hand only, to the next player on his team. The team to finish first wins.

CIRCUS HOOPS RACE

FOR BOYS AND GIRLS   2 TO 8 PLAYERS   PLAYED INDOORS
ELEMENTARY—JR. HIGH   INDIVID.—TEAM   OR OUTDOORS

The equipment required for this game is twelve strong paper plates 9 inches in diameter, two small, round balloons, and two short flat sticks or spatulas to be used as balloon drivers. The plates will serve for eight players, but each player needs the number of balloons and spatulas mentioned.

The balloons should be blown up to 4 inches in diameter. It is best to have pairs of balloons of the same color and a few pairs of different colors, for instance, two red balloons, two blue, or two yellow, in order to distinguish more easily between two players or two teams. The spatulas or flat sticks should be from 6 inches to 1 foot in length and about 1 inch wide, more or less. The longer drivers provide the most fun and difficulty. A 6-inch circle is cut out of the exact center of

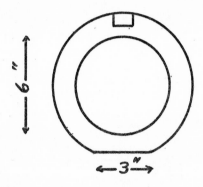

each of eight paper plates, leaving a 1½-inch rim all around. The eight plates are hinged in pairs, with pieces of strong paper or cotton cloth 2 inches square. A hinge is pasted over the outside edge of each two hoops and comes down about 1 inch outside of each plate. The hinged part of the hoop is the top and the two plates can easily be spread 2 or 3 inches apart at the bottom, which should be squared off a little so that each pair of hinged hoops can stand easily on the ground. The diagram shows what a completed hoop looks like. Should *strong* paper plates not be available for hoops, after the centers of the plates have been cut out, two rims may be pasted together, one fitted inside the other, so that four plates, instead of two, are used for each hinged hoop.

The hoops are set up (see diagram, page 204), with hoops 1 and 4 facing the start and finish plate at each end. Hoops 2 and 3 face sideways. Two inflated balloons are put in each starting plate and a player stands beside each plate, holding a driving stick. On the word "Go!" each player drives one balloon forward, through the nearest hoop, and continues driving the balloon through each hoop, in any order and from either side, until the balloon is driven into the finish plate at the opposite end, which will be empty until the first balloon is driven into it. The player then runs back for the second balloon and drives it through the hoops as before. Should a balloon or driving stick knock over a hoop during the race, the player who knocked it over must set it up in the exact position again and then go back one hoop, as a penalty, driving the balloon through it again before returning to the hoop which was knocked over.

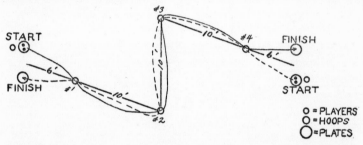

The chance that the players may meet at some point between or even at a hoop adds to the fun and excitement. The first player to arrive at the hoop in such cases should be given the courtesy of the first chance to drive his balloon through.

Played as a team event, the race is run in relay fashion. The first player to complete the course touches off the next player on his team.

This game can be made more difficult by adding additional balloons or hoops and increasing the distance between hoops.

PARTNER BALLOON BOUNCE

FOR BOYS AND GIRLS	4 TO 16 PLAYERS	PLAYED OUTDOORS
ELEMENTARY—JR. HIGH	PARTNER—TEAM	OR INDOORS

This is an amusing game which is best played on calm days. The only equipment needed is one big balloon inflated to

about 10 inches and two paper-plate markers 9 inches in diameter, for each team of two partners. A starting marker is
placed on the ground and another marker placed directly
opposite it 30 feet away, for each team. There should be a
6-foot lane between teams.

The partners stand side by side beside the starting plate and
join hands, the right hand of one partner holding the left
hand of the other. An even better way of joining the partners
is to use a 12-inch length of stout cord or rope, knotted at each
end. They hold this cord between them, one partner holding
the rope directly beside the knot with the right hand, while
the other partner holds it in the same way in the left hand.
On the word "Go!" the two partners keep the cord stretched
between them and drive the balloon, which has been given
to each team, from one to the other, using only the free hand.
They try to keep the balloon bouncing forward toward the
second marker without letting it touch the ground. Each partner must bounce the balloon only once each time it is bounced
between them. Every time a balloon is dropped it must be
picked up and driven forward from where it fell. When the
second marker is reached, the partners change places and the
cord is changed from one hand to the other, so that the partner
who batted the balloon with the right hand on the way to the
second marker will pat it back to the starting marker with the
left hand. The first team to arrive back at the original starting
point wins.

This is another game which makes a good relay race. With
two pairs of partners on a team, the second pair of partners
wait at the second marker and immediately the first pair
arrive at the marker, not before, they take over the cord and
balloon and race back to the starting point. Instead of the
second pair of partners waiting at the second marker, they
may wait at the first marker and start their run from that
point, returning to the starting point again after they have
raced to the second marker. In this way, each pair of partners
will make a complete run from the starting point back to the
starting point. When there are three or four pairs of partners

on each relay team, each pair touches off the next when the
run is completed.

THREE TO ONE

FOR BOYS AND GIRLS   3 TO 12 PLAYERS   PLAYED INDOORS
ELEMENTARY—JR. HIGH   INDIVID.—TEAM   OR OUTDOORS

Players form triangles of three players, each player forming
a point of the triangle and standing 8 feet away from the other
two players. The only equipment needed for this game is a
balloon 8 to 12 inches in diameter when inflated, for each trio.
All players face toward the center of the triangle.

On the word "Go!" one player drives the balloon up into the
air with the palm of one hand, directing it toward either of
the other two players. The one to whom it is bounced drives
it to the third player, who has not yet had a chance to bat the
balloon. That player bounces it to the player who started the
game. No sequence of strikes is required but no player must
strike the balloon twice in succession. Each player must remember this when driving the balloon to another person on
his team, as a player who strikes it twice in succession loses
the match for his team when it is competing against another
triangle. The team which keeps the balloon longest in the air
is the winner.

In individual play, the player who has to strike the balloon
twice in order to drive it forward, or who fails to drive it so
that it may be easily struck by the player to whom it is driven,
drops out of the game, and the two remaining players carry
on until one is forced out of the game.

BALLOON BOWLING

FOR BOYS AND GIRLS   3 TO 12 PLAYERS   PLAYED OUTDOORS
ELEMENTARY—JR. HIGH   INDIVID.—TEAM   OR INDOORS

The equipment needed for this game is five small, round
balloons which inflate to about 4 inches and four paper saucers
6 inches in diameter, for each player or each team of three or

four players. Like most balloon games, this one is best played indoors when there is a breeze blowing.

Four saucers are placed on the ground 8 feet apart, in a straight line. A balloon is placed on each saucer, and a fifth balloon is given to the player who stands 3 feet behind the first saucer at the starting end. There should be two or more lanes of saucers, each one set up in the same way, with a space of 3 feet between lanes.

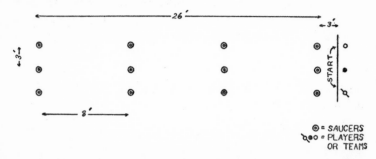

⊚ = SAUCERS
ⱷ◦ = PLAYERS
    OR TEAMS

When the leader says "Bowl!" each player bowls his balloon at the balloon in the first saucer in line. He tries to knock the balloon out of that saucer with the balloon he bowls, and his hand must not be on it when it strikes the balloon from the saucer. The balloon which was used to bowl with must be rolled into the empty saucer and remain there, before the player may continue to bowl with the balloon which was knocked out of the saucer. Using the balloon knocked from the first saucer, he goes on to the second balloon in line, which he bowls from its saucer. He continues as before to the next balloon in line. When a player has bowled all of the balloons correctly from each saucer, he runs with the fifth balloon back to the starting point. The first one to arrive back wins the match.

When teams bowl, the players of each team stand one behind the other. The second player on the team begins to bowl when the fifth balloon is handed to him by the first player. The third player is touched off by the second player, and so it continues until all members of the team have bowled.

Balloon Bowling may also be played with the teams divided so that there are equal numbers at each end of the line of balloons. In this version the second player begins to bowl with the fifth balloon as soon as the first player reaches the finish end of the line.

TRY-ANGLES

FOR BOYS AND GIRLS	5 TO 12 PLAYERS	PLAYED OUTDOORS
ELEMENTARY—JR. HIGH	PARTNER	OR INDOORS

Each team of two partners requires three round balloons inflated to about 4 inches in diameter, two paper-plate markers 6 inches in diameter, and a player who stands with legs apart in a feet-astride position and hands on his hips, forming the three triangles required for the game.

Two paper plates are placed on the ground 30 feet apart, one plate being directly behind the other. Three balloons are put in the starting plate. The player who forms the triangles stands 20 feet directly behind the starting plate. The lanes for each team should be 4 feet apart.

On the "Go!" signal, the partners hit one of their balloons into the air, pat it to the player who forms the triangles and gently tap it between his legs. Once the balloon has been bounced between the legs triangle, without touching the ground, it is kept in the air and driven through the angle formed by the right arm, then through the triangle made by the left arm, after which it is kept in the air until it is patted into the finish plate. The partners then race back for the second balloon and continue the race against the other teams until all three balloons are in the finish plate. The balloons must not be allowed to touch the ground at any time. If one does so, the team must drive it directly back into the starting plate and recommence from that point as a forfeit. The team which finishes correctly first is the winner.

Try-Angles can also be played with each team racing in any way it wishes. For instance, the partners of a team may each drive a balloon, instead of bouncing one between them, and the three balloons may be driven through the angles in any order. The risk of stunting in order to try to gain time is borne by each team because every balloon which touches the ground has to be raced directly back to the starting plate as a forfeit and driven over again.

MEDLEY BALLOON TENNIS

FOR BOYS AND GIRLS	2 TO 8 PLAYERS	PLAYED OUTDOORS
JR. HIGH—SR. HIGH	INDIVID.—TEAM	OR INDOORS

This new balloon game was originally created by the author as an activity requiring concentration and quickness of movement, but it is added to this book, along with other brand-new balloon games, because in the world of play today there are so many balloons and so few balloon games.

The simple equipment required for the game is four white paper plates 9 inches in diameter, glued in pairs one inside the other to reinforce them. This makes two rackets. Two paper-plate markers 6 inches in diameter and a balloon measuring about 8 inches in diameter when inflated are also needed. This outfits two players. The markers are placed directly opposite each other, 8 feet apart, and a player stands behind each marker, facing his opponent.

The underhand stroke should be used throughout the game and the medley strokes sequence closely observed. To start the game, a player serves the balloon by a straight-forward bounce with his racket so that it travels fairly high and straight to the opposite marker. His opponent returns the balloon in exactly the same way. The first player again serves as before, but this time his opponent spins completely around by the right when he sees the balloon is served—and not before. He ends his spin facing the first player, to whom he returns the balloon by a simple forward stroke. It is now the first player who spins completely around by the right, before returning the balloon. This time his opponent spins completely around by the left before driving the balloon back, and it is returned in the same way, after a left spin by the first player.

Now the opponent spins around *twice* before sending the balloon back, and it is returned to him in the same way. The game then continues as it started, using the straight-forward bounce again, and it proceeds as before.

Each player who lets the balloon fall to the ground, returns or receives it in the wrong way, or has to use an extra stroke to return it loses 2 points for each fault. One point is also deducted for each serve which is too low or too high or too wide of the marker for an opponent to reach it fairly easily. Any player who loses 10 points, or the number decided before the match begins, loses the game.

This game can also be played as a team game, with two on each team. The leader who directs the game can add whatever other fancy serves he chooses.

BOUNCER

FOR BOYS AND GIRLS   4 TO 12 PLAYERS   PLAYED INDOORS
ELEMENTARY—JR. HIGH   INDIVID.—TEAM   OR OUTDOORS

The only gear required for this game is two strong, round balloons of different colors inflated to at least 7 inches. They will bounce best when almost fully blown up, when a knot may be tied in the neck of the balloon and the end cut off. Two squares are marked on the floor or on very smooth ground, one square inside the other. The outer square measures 6 feet, and the inner one 3 feet.

A player stands just outside the edge of the bigger square, as shown in the diagram. In the partner version, for older players, the two partners stand opposite each other, one on each side of the square. Each player remains in his original position throughout the game. Each set of partners is given a balloon; on the word "Go!" they start to bounce the balloon on the floor between them across the square. A player should not strike the balloon twice in succession during its one-way trip across the square. Inside the inner square lies the danger zone, since the object of the game is for each pair of partners to bounce their rivals' balloon out of the 3-foot inner square by hitting it with a rebound bounce, from the floor only. Balloons must not be thrown but bounced, with one hand only, throughout the game. A partner-team scores 5 points each time it bounces a rival balloon out of the inner square. Partners lose 2 points for letting their balloons "die" inside either square, and 2 points for touching a rival balloon with a hand. The leader must see that both partner-teams bounce their

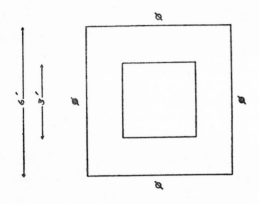

= PARTNERS

balloons fairly continuously and not hold back until the rival balloon is bounced in the square a few times. The winning score may be set at 20 or 30 points. For younger players, or less skillful older ones, the balloon may be bounced by hand, without rebound from the floor, directly against the rival balloon.

In team play, two or three members of a team face two or three members of the same team across the square. The players on each team bounce their team's balloon whenever they get a chance, but not more than twice in succession. In this form of the game each team may be given two balloons, each team having balloons of different colors. The two additional balloons complicate rather than simplify matters, but they add to the fun.

14.

Active Games for Little Folk

HOW ABOUT ME?

FOR BOYS AND GIRLS   3 TO 14 PLAYERS   PLAYED OUTDOORS
PRIMARY   INDIVIDUAL   OR INDOORS

This game tests the self-control and alertness of young players and teaches the value of rules.

The leader marks a circle on the ground from 20 to 40 feet in diameter, according to the number of players and the play space available. In the center of this circle, another, 10 feet in diameter, is marked and paper-plate markers 6 inches in diameter are stapled to the ground about 4 feet apart and arranged as shown in the diagram or in a zigzag pattern. There must be one marker less than the number of players.

The players stand at least an arm's length apart just outside the big circle, facing around the circle in the same direction. On the command, "Walk around the circle," the players do so. In a moment or so, the command is, "Knees up," and the players walk with their knees raised to waist level with each step. On the words, "Turn about," the players turn around and walk around the circle in the opposite direction. The leader may also use commands such as, "Both hands above head," "Arms folded," and similar ones. The leader then says, "Stop! turn your backs to the center of the circle. Now move around sideways at a walk, to the right." When the players are following the various commands correctly, the leader suddenly calls, "Go!" at which the players must *walk fast*, but not run, to the center of the circle and stand with a foot on any marker. Only one player is allowed to each marker and the first player to

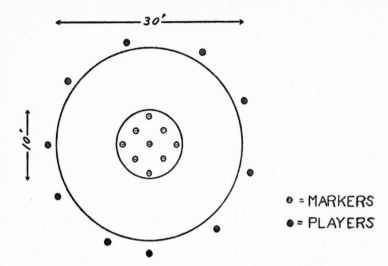

⊖ = MARKERS

● = PLAYERS

get his foot on it is a winner and continues the next round. A player without a marker or one who runs to the markers instead of walking is ruled out of the game. One or more markers are removed so that once again there is one marker less than the number of players remaining, and the game starts again. The last remaining player or players win.

To test the alertness of the players, the leader may give the "Go!" signal at any time as the players move around the circle.

THE THREE BEARS

FOR BOYS AND GIRLS   7 TO 18 PLAYERS   PLAYED OUTDOORS
PRIMARY   INDIVIDUAL   OR INDOORS

Three bears are apparently asleep in the middle of a 30-foot-in-diameter circle which has been marked on the ground. The other players move around outside the circle and, from time to time, try to go as close to the sleeping bears as they dare, because they know that bears wake up easily in summer —and in winter too when they are disturbed. Suddenly, one or more bears wake up and chase the daring players who have ventured closest, in an effort to tag as many as possible before they can escape to safety outside the circle. All players who are tagged are out of the game, and the last three to be tagged take the place of the bears for the next round. When players hesitate for too long a period before entering the bears' den, the leader may call out, "All into the bears' den!" whereupon every player must enter the circle, giving the bears a chance to go to work on the intruders who so rudely disturb their sleep. The bears may run on two legs or crawl.

The game is more exciting and amusing when only one bear wakes up on the first invasion of the den, scrambles lazily onto all fours, and then lies down and goes to sleep again. The players are sure that he sleeps because he snores. Such tactics will decoy more players into the den for the second time, when all three bears may rush them. One bear can pretend to be very lazy and slow-moving until his chance to strike at close quarters comes along. He may sit snoring, with wagging, nodding head and tightly closed eyes, only to awake with startling suddenness when a player comes too close to him.

Leaders may use fewer or more bears, depending on the number of the players and the size of the circle used. More fun can be added by having mother, father, and baby bear—who is far faster than his size indicates—guard the circle from outsiders.

FROG RACE

FOR BOYS AND GIRLS	4 TO 16 PLAYERS	PLAYED OUTDOORS
PRIMARY	INDIVID.—TEAM	

This amusing race requires only a paper ball for each player. The ball is made from three double sheets of a standard-size newspaper, rolled up hard, and they will last longer and give less trouble if they are tied together firmly with string. Two lines are marked on the ground directly opposite each other and 30 feet apart.

For the individual race, all of the players line up directly behind one of the lines. When the leader says "Get ready!" each player places the paper ball between his ankles, and he must not touch it with his hands as he hops. The first player to reach the second line wins. When a ball falls from between the ankles, the player to whom it belongs must pick it up, hop back two hops, place the ball between his ankles again, and continue the race.

The race may be run either with the hands clasped around and just below the knees or with the arms folded, which is the hardest way for the players. When a longer and more varied hop is desired, the players may hop with arms around knees to the second line and return with folded arms to the starting point.

Double Frog Race will cause even more fun, as players team up so that each player has a partner. One hops directly in front of the other with the hands of the player behind holding the shoulders of the player in front. Both players hold a ball between the ankles, and each must stop when either ball becomes displaced.

When either of these frog races is played as a relay, each team should be divided into two sections, one of which lines up behind either of the lines. When the first player arrives at the second line, he touches off the next player, who races back to the start, and the game continues in this way until each team member has had a turn.

CRAB CRAWL RACE

FOR BOYS AND GIRLS   2 TO 14 PLAYERS   PLAYED OUTDOORS
PRIMARY   INDIVID.—TEAM

This is another game to be played on grass—grass inspected to be sure that there are no stones or other obstacles to cause hazards. Two lines are marked on the ground opposite each other and 30 feet apart. These lines can be marked with white tape or by paper-plate markers, as detailed in Chapter 3. The players go down on hands and knees so that their bodies are sideways to the starting line, with a distance of 3 feet between players. On the word "Go!" they race on hands and knees, sideways, to the second line, where the first arrival wins. Should two players arrive at the same time, the tie may be broken by the players racing back to the starting line in the same manner as before.

Teams of two or more players can compete against other teams with the same number of players. The event can also be carried out as a relay race, with half of each team waiting, to be touched off one by one, at each line.

POP UPS

FOR BOYS AND GIRLS   4 TO 16 PLAYERS   PLAYED OUTDOORS
PRIMARY   INDIVIDUAL   OR INDOORS

The players crouch in a circle about 30 feet in diameter. The leader stands in the center of it, holding a balloon which should measure from 8 to 12 inches in diameter. She throws the balloon high into the air, calling out the name of a player as she does so. That player "pops up," rushes to the center of the circle and hits the balloon up into the air three times, with the palm of the hand, without changing place before squatting down again. Should the balloon fall to the ground before the player reaches it, or while being hit into the air three times, the player missing it is out of the game. A player who catches the balloon instead of hitting it is also out of the game, and catching it is a temptation which some players find difficult to resist.

BALLOON BLOW

FOR BOYS AND GIRLS   2 TO 10 PLAYERS   PLAYED OUTDOORS
PRIMARY   INDIVID.—TEAM

This is a race in which each player or team requires two paper-plate markers 6 inches in diameter and a round balloon which is at least 6 inches in diameter when inflated. The markers at the starting end are laid on the ground in a straight line 4 feet apart, and another series of plate markers is placed directly opposite them at a distance of 30 feet. A play area of inspected grass is best for this game.

Each player kneels behind a plate at the starting end and holds his balloon on it until the leader says "Go!" Then, moving on hands and knees, each player blows his balloon to and into the plate marker on the finish line. The balloon must not be touched with the hands during the race; any player who

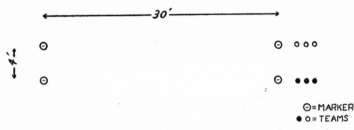

does so is either ruled out of the game or sent back 6 feet as a penalty. The distance crawled in this game can be doubled by having the players race back from the finish line to the starting point, after their balloons have actually been put into the plate at the second line. The player finishing first, provided he has not touched his balloon with his hands, is the winner.

Teams of two or more players on each team can play this game in relay race form by having half of the team stand behind one marker, while the other half of the team stands behind the other marker. When one player has blown the balloon onto the plate on the second line, the next player blows it from there back onto the plate at the starting point. Each player touches off the other until all have had a turn.

HEADS

FOR BOYS AND GIRLS	4 TO 10 PLAYERS	PLAYED OUTDOORS
PRIMARY	INDIVIDUAL	OR INDOORS

A line is marked on the ground, or markers are used to indicate the starting line. Another line is marked on the ground directly opposite about 30 feet distant. Each player is given a big round balloon inflated to about 8 inches or more in diameter. Each player lines up behind the starting line and on the word "Go!" butts the balloon with his head to the finish line. Players must not touch the balloons with their hands or arms, and when a balloon falls to the ground the player must not touch it until it actually lands. The player then picks it up, steps back 2 paces, and starts to butt the balloon again from that point. The first player to arrive at the finish line still bouncing the balloon on his head wins. Older players can be asked to turn around, still bouncing the balloons on their heads, at the second line and return in the same manner to the starting point.

The smallest players can have their own race in which they strike the balloons with their hands instead of using their heads to propel them.

Heads is a game for the outdoors only on breezeless days. In Chapter 13, full details for inflating balloons and using them to advantage when there is a slight breeze are given to help novice leaders.

ROUND YOU GO!

FOR BOYS AND GIRLS	8 TO 20 PLAYERS	PLAYED OUTDOORS
PRIMARY	INDIVIDUAL	OR INDOORS

The players stand in a circle with their legs astride and a distance of 3 feet between players. The players all face toward the center of the circle and stand in an easy, comfortable position, though they have their legs apart to form bridges.

A paper-plate marker 6 inches in diameter is placed on the ground between any two players in the circle. These two players, one on each side of the marker, go down on hands and knees, facing in opposite directions with their toes just touching the marker.

On the word "Go!" these two players race in opposite directions, on hands and knees, beneath the bridges formed by the legs of the other players and back to the starting point. The player who first places both hands on the marker is the winner. The players compete by twos until all have had a chance to race.

Extra fun and excitement occurs at the point in the circle where the two players meet. If a player has his head through a bridge, the other player must give him right of way; if they arrive at a bridge at exactly the same moment, who gets through the bridge first may have to be decided by a little shouldering, but with both hands and knees on the ground. The leader should keep an eye open to see that things go smoothly when two players meet head-on.

INDOOR BUFF

FOR BOYS AND GIRLS	6 TO 12 PLAYERS	PLAYED INDOORS
PRIMARY	INDIVIDUAL	OR OUTDOORS

One player is blindfolded. His ears are left uncovered. He stands in the middle of a large room, with cleared floor space. The other players form a tight circle around him until told to spread out. Once in position, which they choose for themselves, they must remain motionless and quiet. The blindfolded player then faces in any direction he likes, takes 5 paces forward in that direction and stops. He stretches out his hands in any direction and tries to touch someone. Should he touch one or more players, the first one touched is blindfolded for the next game; but should he touch nobody, he must try again in the next game.

Although the players, once they have taken up their positions, cannot change places or even move out of their places, they can stoop down or lean backward or forward to avoid the groping hands of the blindfolded player.

BACKWARD CRAWL RACE

FOR BOYS AND GIRLS	4 TO 10 PLAYERS	PLAYED OUTDOORS
PRIMARY	INDIVIDUAL	

The racers remove their shoes and line up on the grass, which has been carefully checked in advance to be certain that there are no stones or other objects in the play area. The players kneel with their fingers just touching a line marked on the ground with a piece of white tape or gauze bandage. The players should be about 3 feet apart. *Behind* them about 30 feet distant is another line to which they must race backward on hands and knees without looking round on the way. On the word "Go!" the race is on, and the players will find that it is no easy task to race backward in a straight line. The first player to reach the finish line wins, or when all of the racers are off course, the one nearest to the line is the winner. To make a longer race, the players may be asked to turn around at the second line and race back again.

LOLLIPOP HUNT

FOR GIRLS AND BOYS   6 TO 16 PLAYERS   PLAYED OUTDOORS
PRIMARY   INDIVIDUAL

This is another race to be played on a patch of grass which has been previously inspected carefully. The leader may either mark a circle 30 feet in diameter on the ground or have the players stand in the form of a circle of about the same size. They face outward and then go down on hands and knees with their feet pointing toward the middle of the circle. Unless they are all wearing sneakers, it is wise to have the players remove their boots or shoes before the hunt begins. Each player is blindfolded with a strip of cloth, or his head is covered with a clean brown paper bag which has not been worn by another player. The sanitary methods of blindfolding are detailed in Chapter 4. As soon as the players are blindfolded, half a dozen wrapped lollipops are placed on the ground close to the center of the circle. There should be at least 2 feet between lollipops.

When the "Hunt!" signal is given, the players crawl backward toward the middle of the circle and grope for the candies. The player who gets the most is the winner.

HOOP BALL

FOR BOYS AND GIRLS	4 TO 20 PLAYERS	PLAYED OUTDOORS
PRIMARY	INDIVID.—TEAM	OR INDOORS

The equipment needed is a metal hoop, or a wooden hoop, about 18 or 20 inches in diameter with a rim about 1 inch wide. In all games where metal hoops are used the rims should be carefully wrapped around with insulating tape or cloth to cover any sharp edges. A hoop made of wood can usually be sandpapered so that it is made perfectly smooth. In addition to the hoop, four or more tennis balls, or similar soft rubber balls, are required. Volleyballs, soccer balls, or basketballs are also suitable and cause more fun.

The players stand around a circle marked on the ground, 15 or 20 feet distant from the hoop, which is placed flat on the ground directly in the middle of the circle. The players take turns at rolling the balls so that they go into the hoop and remain inside. The balls which remain inside are taken out and credit is given to the players who put them in. Two or more players may roll balls at the same time, but no player should roll a ball twice in succession and all players should be given an equal chance to compete. Instead of removing the ball from inside the hoop as soon as it has been rolled in, it may be left in until two or three balls remain inside the hoop. When a ball is knocked out of the hoop by another ball, the ball knocked outside does not score, unless the leader decides that it may do so. The winner is the player who first puts three balls, rolled at any time during one game, into the hoop.

When only four players, or even two, play, the game may be played with the hoop placed on the ground between two lines marked 30 feet apart. Half of the players stand on each line and they may roll the balls at any time and in any order. The simple rules are the same as those used when the game is played in circle formation.

Teams, with the same number of players on each side, may compete, with each team standing in a certain part of the circle. Each team may be assigned to one half or one quarter of the circle, according to whether there are two or four teams playing.

WILLIAM TELL

FOR BOYS AND GIRLS   2 TO 6 PLAYERS   PLAYED OUTDOORS
PRIMARY   INDIVIDUAL   OR INDOORS

Each player starts from a line marked on the ground, opposite which there is another line marked 30 feet away. Instead of marking lines on the ground the leader may mark the position of these lines by stapling paper-plate markers on the ground, one to indicate each end of the line. The players are each given an apple to be balanced on the head during the race.

On the word "Go!" each player balances the apple on his head and takes one forward step toward the left with the left foot, then one forward step toward the right with the right foot. Players continue to advance in this way until the finish line is reached. Should the apple fall from a player's head as he walks, he may be retired from the game, or he may be allowed to place the apple on his head again and continue the race.

A variation of this game, for players with a good sense of balance, is the cross step advance. At the start, the forward step toward the left is made with the right foot and the forward step toward the right is made with the left foot. This cross step continues throughout the race. In either of the above methods, when the players develop skill, they can be asked to turn around when the second line is reached and return to the starting point, thus doubling the distance covered during the race.

HIPPETY-HOP

FOR GIRLS AND BOYS   2 TO 8 PLAYERS   PLAYED OUTDOORS
PRIMARY   INDIVIDUAL   OR INDOORS

This is a hopping race. The leader marks a start and finish line 30 feet apart. The players should stand about 4 feet apart to avoid bumping into each other.

On the word "Go!" each player stoops down, clasps his fingers in front of his ankles, and hops in that position to the second line, where he turns and hops back to the starting point. Should a player lose balance, he must stop, get into the correct position, and then continue the race. The first player to finish wins.

15.

Quiet Games for Little Folk

JOHNNY APPLESEED'S SEEDS

FOR BOYS AND GIRLS   4 TO 16 PLAYERS   PLAYED OUTDOORS
PRIMARY   INDIVIDUAL   OR INDOORS

The leader places a big, bright, burnished apple on a saucer in front of the group. Each player is given a slip of paper and a pencil. They are then told something about Johnny Appleseed and their debt to him, and are asked to write down how many seeds they think there are in the apple, and their color.

When the players have had time to think and each one has written down his guess, and his initials, the slips of paper are collected and the leader goes to work on the apple. The core should be cut out carefully, without peeling the apple, and the seeds placed in the saucer. The player whose guess is closest to the actual number of seeds in the apple wins and gets the apple. In the case of a tie the apple is divided.

HAT SHOP

FOR GIRLS	2 TO 12 PLAYERS	PLAYED INDOORS
PRIMARY	INDIVIDUAL	OR OUTDOORS

This is an interesting and amusing game for girls. The only things needed before the hat shop opens for business are a few sheets of brightly colored tissue or crepe paper, a few pairs of scissors with rounded points, some paste or half a dozen or more small safety pins about 1 inch long, for each would-be milliner.

With a little advice from the leader, if asked for, the hat shop will soon be in operation as the girls cut, paste, or pin together the "creations" which are tried on the head either of the maker or of a model.

The milliner who turns out the most stylish hat and matches the colors in the most becoming way is declared the best hatmaker.

FAIRY TALE FOLK

FOR GIRLS AND BOYS	3 TO 16 PLAYERS	PLAYED OUTDOORS
PRIMARY	INDIVIDUAL	OR INDOORS

This game for younger players is similar to Waxworks, to be found in Chapter 4. In this game the players do not need to remain motionless, unless they wish to. They may even make little motions and noises to help the other players to guess correctly, but this should be done only when the guessers are ready to "give up."

One or two players, when two fairy folk are involved, are chosen to represent "Fairy Tale Folk." The other players are asked to close their eyes until the fairy folk are ready. On the word "Look!" what the guessers are supposed to see may depend a good deal on their imagination. The player or players who are the make-believe fairy folk may be posing as Humpty Dumpty, Rumpelstiltskin, The Sleeping Beauty, Little Miss Muffett, Jack and the Beanstalk, Puss in Boots, Cinderella, Hansel and Gretel, or any other characters in well-known fairy tales.

The players who do the guessing may have three guesses each, but not one after another, and only say their guesses aloud when pointed to by the leader. The leader selects the one to guess first by asking for a display of hands. The player who guesses correctly first is given the next chance to be one of the folk from fairyland. Should nobody guess correctly and the impersonators have done a good job, they are given the chance to pose a second time. Few or no props should be allowed in this game, as they frequently prove a source of delay without adding greatly to the impersonation and they sometimes discourage initiative and imagination on the part of both actors and guessers.

JOIN IN MY SONG

FOR GIRLS AND BOYS	2 TO 12 PLAYERS	PLAYED OUTDOORS
PRIMARY	INDIVIDUAL	OR INDOORS

In this musical game the leader, or a player who is musically inclined, hums a measure or two of a well-known tune. When he stops, the players continue from the point where he stopped, showing that the tune is familiar to them. The players who fail to recognize the tune three times running are out of the game. The last remaining player is the winner and may be given the next chance to lead. A leader or player who can play a variety of tunes on a mouth organ, concertina, or guitar can replace the humming musician. This music session in the form of a game can be made easy for the younger players by using simple nursery rhyme tunes, such as "Three Blind Mice," "Hickory-Dickory-Dock" and similar songs. For a more musically inclined group, tunes from selections such as *Peter and the Wolf*, and songs such as "America the Beautiful," "Waltzing Matilda," "The Blue Tail Fly," "Mandalay," and "The Paddle Song" can be introduced. Airs from Gilbert and Sullivan and other popular operettas are often speedily recognized and well received.

CUP KICK

FOR BOYS AND GIRLS	4 TO 16 PLAYERS	PLAYED OUTDOORS
PRIMARY	INDIVID.—TEAM	OR INDOORS

The only gear required for this game is a big, soft rubber ball and three paper cups, which can be colored brightly. A circle 20 feet in diameter is marked on the ground. The three cone-shaped drinking cups are placed in the form of a triangle in the middle of the circle, with 18 inches between the cups.

The players, or teams of players, take turns at kicking the ball from just outside the circle in an endeavor to knock the cups over. Each cup which is knocked over or moved more than 12 inches from its place scores for the player or team making the kick and is removed from the circle, until only the last cup remains. The player or team knocking over the most cups is the winner, or 5 points can be awarded for each cup put out of business and the score set at 15 points to win.

TOYLAND

FOR BOYS AND GIRLS	6 TO 16 PLAYERS	PLAYED OUTDOORS
PRIMARY	INDIVIDUAL	OR INDOORS

The leader pretends to be the manager of a big toy factory that is turning our presents for next Christmas. Santa Claus is

soon going to visit the factory to order his gifts for the children. The trouble, the leader points out, is that there are no
gifts ready to show Santa as samples. Perhaps if the boys and
girls in the group pretend that they are different toys, the
buyer may give the factory a nice order. The leader gives the
players a few minutes to decide on which toys they wish to be.
The players may imitate by motions, sounds, or both, any toy
which they think the buyer may like, and the group must
represent as many different toys as possible. Two players may
act together if they think they can do a better imitation that
way—perhaps pretending to be Jack and Jill or Hansel and
Gretel. The players must not "dress up," though they may use
scarves or anything that is handy to help the effect.

When the players run out of ideas the leader may suggest
such things as dolls, a top, cowboy, Indian, drum, music box,
rabbit, horse, toy soldier, jack-in-the-box, frog, dog, wrist
watch, or cuckoo clock, to mention a few possibilities. Should
some leaders think that some of the articles suggested are too
difficult to imitate, they underestimate the ingenuity of children. A child who decides to be a wrist watch will grasp her
toes with her fingers to form the wristband and then *tick*
more busily than the busiest wrist watch. The cuckoo clock
child will raise her arms, with the finger tips touching, above
her head to form the pointed top of the clock and her mouth
will open round at short intervals to let the cuckoo sound
come out, to positively identify her as a cuckoo clock.

When the buyer arrives, the leader has the toys "perform." The buyer adds to the fun by being fairly critical of some of the toys, perhaps the ones putting on the best show, and praising the special merits of others who are staging a not-too-good best. All of the toys have been especially warned not to laugh or the buyer will know at once that they are not genuine toys. This gives the buyer a good opportunity to tickle some noses and poke some ribs in the course of the inspection and while winding up some of the toys which have run down. A good buyer, with sympathy and imagination, can provide at least half of the fun produced in Toyland.

Any toy which the buyer can identify right away, by naming it, is bought and taken to one side of the room. Other toys harder to identify but putting on a really good show are also selected for Santa Claus; and when the inspection is over, the buyer asks the most lifelike of the toys bought to give a repeat performance.

NURSERY RHYMING

FOR GIRLS AND BOYS	2 TO 16 PLAYERS	PLAYED INDOORS
PRIMARY	INDIVIDUAL	OR OUTDOORS

The leader quotes two to four of the first words of the first line of a nursery rhyme, and the player who first raises a hand to show that he knows which rhyme is being quoted is asked to recite the rest of the verse. Simple rhymes such as "Baa, Baa, Black Sheep," "Hi Diddle Diddle," "To Market, to Market," and "Jack be Nimble" should not be quoted from the beginning, as it reveals the rhyme immediately. Such quotes have to be started a little farther on, though that is almost equally revealing in some of them. Less-know rhymes such as "As I was going to St. Ives" and many others of the sort can be used for more advanced rhymsters.

If players like Nonsense Rhymes, and most of them do, they may also be used in this little game.

LET'S PLANT A GARDEN

FOR BOYS AND GIRLS   2 TO 20 PLAYERS   PLAYED INDOORS
PRIMARY   INDIVIDUAL   OR OUTDOORS

The scope of this game and of Let's Pack a Trunk, which follows, is limited only by the players' imagination and knowledge. Leaders may add other projects; there are many suitable ones for both girls and boys or mixed groups.

The players vote on the sort of garden which they wish to plant. It may be a flower garden, a vegetable garden, or perhaps a garden in which both vegetables and flowers flourish. The third choice affords the "gardeners" greater scope. In this game, too, the players' imagination can be given free rein. Should a younger player wish to plant potatoes and bananas next to each other, his suggestion can be given consideration. The players may learn a good deal when the leader explains why potatoes and bananas, or blueberries and pomegranates, are unlikely to thrive in the same garden and goes on to tell the difference between northern and southern gardens. The flower beds of the imaginary garden will bloom in a blaze of multicolors by the time the amateur gardeners have contributed their blooms to be accepted and planted by the head gardener, the leader.

LET'S PACK A TRUNK

FOR BOYS AND GIRLS   2 TO 20 PLAYERS   PLAYED INDOORS
PRIMARY   INDIVIDUAL   OR OUTDOORS

This game may sound easy after planting a garden but, as the packing proceeds, the task may become no easy one. For instance, if the leader suggests that the players pack "Aunt Matilda's" trunk, the boys may have some difficulty in knowing just what articles to pack. Girl players will also have their troubles when the imaginary trunk of "Uncle John" is packed. Such situations offer considerable scope for humor and the alert leader will not fail to take advantage of it.

Players will learn a great deal when, in imagination, they pack trunks which could be their own for different kinds of holidays and lengths of stay at various places. A trunk may be packed for a stay at camp, or on a farm, or for a visit to some great city where nice clothes are required.

Leaders can think up suitable topics for girls only, such as "Let's Bake a Cake," or for boys only by deciding to build a speedboat or an airplane.

BUBBLE BLOWING FUN. There are many forms of both quiet and active games which can be played by using soap bubbles as the base of the fun. For instance, the players can compete in trying to blow the biggest bubble which can be successfully floated from the pipe or the smallest bubble which can be shaken from the pipe without breaking. Players can also try to make the most bubbles, of any size, come from one dip of the pipe in the bubble solution. Competitions can be held to see which player can blow a bubble of any size the highest or the farthest, or the one which will last longest when dropped from the pipe onto a tablecloth or blanket. Many other forms of bubble blowing fun will suggest themselves to leaders who take up this sport with their groups. Bubble blowing is good fun for children considerably older than the primary group, provided that a really good bubble blowing solution is used, one which toughens bubbles so that they will last for some time and even withstand a buffeting by the breeze before they finally break. As such a solution is the solution for successful bubble blowing fun, here is an excellent bubble blowing mixture.

BUBBLE BLOWING SOLUTION. Fill a pint jar two thirds full of very hot water. Add ¾ tablespoon of Castile soap powder, or very fine shavings of that soap. When Castile soap is not handy, the same amount of lather-making soap flakes can be used. Let the soap dissolve thoroughly before adding 1 heaping tablespoon of glycerine and ½ tablespoon of sugar. Olive oil or vegetable oil may be used as a substitute for glycerine, but they are second choice. A little water color or a few drops of violet, red, or green ink will add to the natural colors of the mixture produced by the soap and glycerine coloration. Additional color is not necessary but can be added from time to time as an experiment when desired. Shake the solution well until all of the ingredients are completely dissolved, then strain it through a cloth. Let this solution cool and do not use until all of the small bubbles have disappeared. With this solution, bubbles will be extra strong and some will last for at least five minutes.

BUBBLE PIPES. White clay pipes with a stubby stem or with half of the long stem snapped off make good bubble blowing pipes. If there are no suitable pipes available when there is a demand for bubbles, it is easy to make a fairly good bubble blowing pipe from a thick soda straw, though thin straws can be used less successfully. Here is how it is done:

Make four slits in one end of the straw. The slits should be about ¾ inch long, one slit on each side of the straw. Double these four pieces back evenly, as shown in the drawing, and you will have a fairly effective, improvised bubble pipe.

WHO AM I?

FOR BOYS AND GIRLS   2 TO 12 PLAYERS   **PLAYED INDOORS**
PRIMARY   INDIVIDUAL   OR OUTDOORS

At the start of this game the leader may ask, "Who am I in a fairy tale?" or "Who am I in a story about pirates?" in order to give all of the players a chance to do a little guessing. Then the scope is limited but the guessing made more difficult by such questions as "Who am I in *Alice in Wonderland?*" or in some other juvenile story. The questions asked by the players in order to identify the character in the shortest possible time are answered by the leader by a simple "Yes" or "No." Questions such as "Are you a boy?" or "Are you a girl?" help to get the game under way, though more pertinent questions such as "Are you the queen?" or "Are you the hero?" may speed things up. Should the leader decide to represent an animal in a story, he can ask, "What am I?" The first player to guess correctly may be given a chance to try his hand as the questioner.

ANIMAL LIKES

FOR BOYS AND GIRLS   2 TO 12 PLAYERS   PLAYED INDOORS
PRIMARY   INDIVIDUAL   OR OUTDOORS

This is an alphabet type of game. The leader says, "I like my squirrel with an S because it is . . ." The players take turns or all guess at the same time to find a suitable word which begins with the letter S, as all of the words used to describe the animals or birds in this game must begin with the first letter in the animal's name. A player may suggest the word *smart* to describe the squirrel. The leader accepts this and asks for further words that are suitable. She must be prepared to allow a little leeway for the younger players who use such words as *squiggly*. After all, a squirrel is a bit squiggly.

The players who prove themselves skillful at suggesting suitable words may be given the chance to become the questioner.

Index